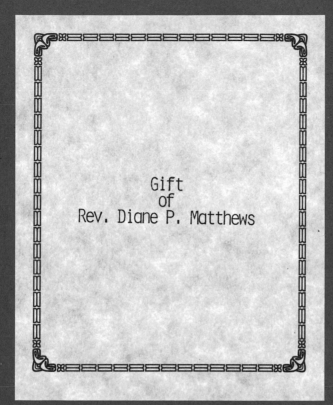

Gift
of
Rev. Diane P. Matthews

Behold, I show you a mystery; We shall not all sleep, but we shall all be changed. . . .

A Woman's Odyssey Toward the Future

The Hunger of Eve

BARBARA MARX HUBBARD

STACKPOLE BOOKS

THE HUNGER OF EVE

Copyright © 1976 by
Barbara Marx Hubbard

Published by
STACKPOLE BOOKS
Cameron and Kelker Streets
P.O. Box 1831
Harrisburg, Pa. 17105

*Published simultaneously in Don Mills, Ontario, Canada by Thomas Nelson &
Sons, Ltd.*

Printed in the U.S.A.

Library of Congress Cataloging in Publication Data
Hubbard, Barbara Marx, 1929–
    The Hunger of Eve.
    Autobiographical.
    1. Hubbard, Barbara Marx, 1929–   I. Title.
CT275.H662A34   973.92′092′4 [B]   76–17267
ISBN 0–8117–0861–6

To all people who have energy to give
to the future of humankind
especially
to the young people building the
New Worlds Center

Phases

I

When I first read Genesis in my youth, I was on Eve's side. I thought she was right to eat the apple of the Tree of Knowledge of Good and Evil—I would have! It was worth the suffering to struggle out of animal innocence to become human. But there was a second tree in the garden that fascinated me even more: the Tree of Life.

Jehovah became very upset because Eve was curious about that second tree; he knew that if she tasted its fruit, the "man" would become "as one of us" and "live forever." The more I read, the more I found myself urging her on—go, Eve, go! I was curious, too, and even then, human consciousness was driving me to reach beyond my narrow self toward some new way of being; I already hungered for the greater meaning of life. But Jehovah drove us out of the garden, and guarded the tree with cherubims and a flaming sword. After all, we were an immature species, too ego-centered and destructive to handle the power.

Now, ready or not, we're reaching for the Tree of Life once

The Hunger Awakens

more, and in some profound way that tree corresponds to the hunger that drove me as a little girl through a comfortable existence, beyond my life as wife and mother of five children, toward participation in this magnificent drama. Somehow the hunger propelled me to a new vantage point, right on center stage with all the rest of humankind, treading either on the very threshold of destruction or into the greatest age in human history.

> *What's the purpose of life*
> *when you have enough things?*

My earliest memory is of standing in a crib, angry, clutching the bars to keep from falling. I had been put to bed early. The afternoon sun was shining brightly in my eyes, and I could hear adult voices talking and laughing somewhere else in the house. I rattled the bars of my crib and cried for them to come and take me out. I was missing something—I wanted to be part of it.

Then there were little incidences—premonitions. Once, riding with my father in his gleaming Rolls-Royce through the streets of Harlem, we stopped at a red light under the Elevated on Second Avenue. It was a cold, ugly, rainy twilight. Faces of young men pressed against the window and glared at us. I reached for my father's hand and held it tightly under the fur rug. I felt the injustice of being in while they were shut out, but, I thought, *they don't know what it feels like to be me, inside, scared; it doesn't feel as good as they think.*

My father, a toy manufacturer, was a strong, vital, successful, self-made man. I was secure in his love. I can still remember the aroma of his cigar, the excitement of being taken to opening nights at the theatre, sledding in Central Park, the fun we had summers on Lazy Day Farm in Connecticut with my brothers and sisters.

Life in New York City felt natural. I was unself-conscious, totally absorbed, and didn't even know I was "happy." Each day I walked home from Dalton School to our Fifth Avenue apartment with a contingent of boys. We played the piano, ate chocolate eclairs, had hose fights on the penthouse, and gossiped endlessly about our friends.

We moved from New York City to a "Gone with the Wind" mansion in Scarsdale when my mother became ill with cancer. I prayed constantly for her to survive this dreadful monster that was devouring her alive. Once I caught a glimpse of the scar on her chest after her first breast was removed. I was horrified and humiliated, shocked at its ugliness in contrast to her beauty. At night I tried desperately to reach God, begging Him to save her, offering my entire being in return for her life. But one evening my father came back from the hospital, and it was over. "Little mother is dead," he explained as gently as possible. Helpless, I collapsed in grief, and he did his best to comfort me. "It's all right to cry," he whispered.

I was crying in his arms when, unexpectedly, a fierce anger

arose from my despair. *No!* I thought. *I will* not *cry! I simply will* not *accept the powerlessness of life against this mindless destruction! I will* not *accept my failure to reach* God! *I will* not *accept that the universe is meaningless or evil!* It was happening—my desire for personal contact with the forces of life was awakening. I was only fourteen, but the real hunger for deeper purpose had begun. My childhood was over.

The social life in Westchester was stultifying and humiliating. My father cared nothing for Scarsdale; his friends and activities were in New York. But if your parents weren't part of the community, you were left out—truly left out. For instance, I was unhappy when I wasn't invited to a dance because we didn't belong to the country club.

"You have no right to be unhappy," my father reminded me. "There are *real* problems—sickness, poverty, war—and then there are man-made problems. Yours are man-made."

My father is a second-generation American. He wanted to sever any ties to the limitations of his past, and he reared his children to be Americans. His message was simply, "Do your best." *At what?* I wondered. My grandmother, Clara Marx, had come to the New World from Austria, aged sixteen, pregnant, with one dollar in her pocket. My grandfather was seventeen, a tailor who had set up shop in Brooklyn in preparation for her arrival. So my father had grown up in Brooklyn with a sense of hope. If you were willing to work, anything was possible. He was one who "made it"—a millionaire at thirty, founder and head of Louis Marx and Company (called the "Henry Ford of the toy business," as one of the first to mass produce toys inexpensively).

I had no idea I was of Jewish ancestry. One day at Rye Country Day School, on a picnic, my class was in a circle, each telling what his or her religion was. When my turn came, I said, "I don't know. I guess I have no religion."

Someone said, "Aren't you Jewish?"

I shook my head. "No, I'm nothing."

One girl responded vehemently, "Well, the Jews murdered Christ!"

I was horrified that she was holding *me* responsible for *that*. Moreover, finding out I was Jewish and that Jews were considered alien was a shock, particularly since I had never set foot in a temple, met a rabbi, or related to the Jewish culture. In fact, I wasn't related by birth to any older tradition, religious or cultural.

The children in our family were very close, perhaps because my father used to make us compete. Louis, eighteen months younger than I, was always teasing us. Once my father made him fight each sister with an arm tied behind his back. Louis hated to lose and would cry bitterly when defeated at any game. Jacqueline, pretty, with a headful of dark, curly hair, promptly bit him through his robe, but Patricia, the youngest, wouldn't hit him; she was gentle and sensitive, cried easily, and loved everyone. I, being the bossy one, told my father the fight was unfair and refused to enter the fray. We were drawn to one another and decided to pay no attention to winning or losing. If my father criticized one of us, the others came to the defense. To this day, anything of importance that one has asked of the other has been immediately and happily given.

Since my father made toys, Christmas played a significant role in our lives. However, we had more toys than anyone could possibly want; I literally lived in a toy culture. But as Christmas approached, my excitement mounted. I wanted it to come, yet didn't, because once we started opening the presents, there would be only a few hours, and then it would be over. Beneath the expectation was the foreknowledge of disappointment. Even worse, I didn't really want those toys. I already had so many that whenever I opened the toy closet, they fell down upon my head.

One Christmas I noticed my father wasn't with us; he was upstairs in his room. I was annoyed and went up to find him working. He was—and is—shaped like Santa Claus: short, portly, bald, with compact strength and a penetrating glance that can frighten or attract.

"What are you working for?" I asked.

"Next Christmas," he said.

I was amazed that anyone could be thinking that far ahead.

But I suspected he was still enjoying the holidays more than I, because he already had something to do for next Christmas. That's when I first sensed that working *for* something was better than being given something. The problem was that I didn't know *what* to work for. My father believed material security was the purpose of work. His motive was never again to be poor, to have to wait at the end of the line, as he put it. But he worried that in giving his children money, he was destroying their motivation. "If I give you this money," he said, "you'll never know the value of a dollar. You'll grow up to be spoiled brats."

"Take it away then," I said. "I don't want to be a spoiled brat."

He shook his head. "That would be false. You'd know if you were *really* starving, I'd pick you up and save you. I'd rather you learn what it's like to waste."

When I went to the movies with friends, he gave me ten dollars rather than five. I was ashamed to have more. In fact, I hid it, or wasted it on candy and then felt sick.

I was determined to find *something* to work for—not more money, however, because I already had more than enough, just as I had too many toys. I was on welfare from my father, but any level of welfare is insufficient without a challenge to engender growth. *What's the purpose of life when you have enough things?* I decided to try to answer that question.

When I was sixteen I joined the Episcopal church and went to Sunday School in Scarsdale at night with a group of adults who were half-dosing in a stuffy church basement. I entered the church because I was seeking some contact more meaningful than the superficial life at Rye Country Day School—some contact, but I didn't know with what. Sunday after Sunday I went to church. Once I prayed so hard I almost fainted, trying to hear a signal from God that He really did exist. I got absolute silence.

Beyond that disappointment, I was deeply irritated with the minister who preached that God was good and man was evil. It seemed to me that Jehovah was more at fault than we. His behavior toward His children was unacceptable. There we were, weak creatures, treated cruelly by a God who had all the characteristics of a tyrant. *It's not true*, I thought. *Man is good. We're not passive children. We're responsible. We must respect ourselves, not hate ourselves.* So I left the Episcopal church.

While I was trying to become an Episcopalian, I actually did become a good student at Rye Country Day School. I love to learn. But I was still looking for challenges—any challenge—so I decided in my senior year to run for student president. My brother, sisters, and all their friends campaigned for me—balloons, posters, cookie and milk strategy meetings. Since I had more siblings than the other candidates, I won. The victory had no meaning, though—I had nothing good to do for the school. After that I never tried to win just to win. Competitiveness diminished in me, even though I came from a very competitive family and really do like to win.

I kept having this uncomfortable feeling that I was missing something. I was graduating from Rye Country Day, and I had had my year as president. I had done well enough at everything to know that more of the same wouldn't suffice; more material goods, more winning, more popularity, wouldn't make any difference. My hunger increased.

---

*How can people live and
not know why they're living?*

I had to select a college. Bryn Mawr was the hardest women's college, I was told, so I chose it. The sense of need and hunger for something "different" was growing. However, there was no cultural affirmation for this unnamed hunger. I wasn't even articulating it to myself clearly, except for certain flashes when I would look up to the universe at night and realize that not only was there a lot going on in *this* world, but there were billions and billions of stars out there, and I felt a part of that. During those flashes, I experienced a joyful sense of unity with the universe. I lost consciousness of Barbara Marx and felt a strange oneness with the stars so far above. The fundamental similarity of our origins and composition, the unity of inanimate and animate, became clear. I couldn't understand why as a species we couldn't put our differences into their obviously superficial places. *What is this centrifugal force that forever pulls against the centripetal force?* I wondered. I couldn't discuss these questions with anyone, so I decided to start a journal, which now includes fifty-five volumes, to keep in touch with this deeper reality, to try to nourish this hunger. I made my first entry on May 27, 1948, at the age of eighteen.

> *I've waited far too long to begin you, my journal. Feelings, intuitions, ideas, have been lost irreparably. I have a desperate need to create. All my life I've absorbed, never once given. By using myself as a catalytic agent I hope to give pattern and form to the mass of sensations that have impressed themselves upon my brain. The power of intelligence is to connect, to relate, and to integrate impressions.*

> *If there's a God, it's He who unites past with present and future, finite with infinite, truth with falsity, until all are more than a conglomeration, until all is one and that one is far greater than the sum of its parts. That oneness is God's creation.*

In looking over the catalog of courses at Bryn Mawr, my heart once again sank with depression. I realized I could easily get more knowledge in any of those fields—literature, history, science, etc. —but they were broken into separate, unrelated courses. We were supposed to select our major when we were still freshmen. There was no way for me to relate these separate boxes of learning to the much more general, profound longing for purpose, for relatedness to all of life.

Joan Auerbach, my roommate, and I were chatting about what we would do after college.

"It would be fun to go to Washington and get a job," she said.

Thinking of nothing better, I agreed. "Why not?"

So we both majored in political science. The method of search for meaningful vocation or avocation at that period was given no significance. You were supposed to "know" what you were interested in, but, in fact, this link between unique talent and society is exceedingly difficult to identify. The courses were dry and detailed. Almost no one was interested in a philosophical search for greater meaning.

I was very unhappy with the normal college dating procedures —blind dates. That's just what they were: blind! When I went out with young men, I asked them, "What's your purpose? What are you working for?" They had never thought about it. It became the great unanswered question. *How can people live and not know why they're living?* I wondered.

I couldn't learn through the general curriculum at Bryn Mawr. The moment of conscious detachment occurred when we were studying Pascal's conversion from a skeptical mathematical genius to a passionate Christian. I read those pages with tremendous excitement. Pascal had found meaning through this conversion—a relationship to Christ, God—an ineffable joy. I went to class in real anticipation of discussing this conversion. Did anyone else feel the *need* for such an experience? Had anyone else *had* such an experience? Was there any way *we* could have it? I raised my hand eagerly to discuss it in terms of our own lives.

The professor just stared at me. "This is *not* a philosophy class, Mademoiselle; it is French literature."

I was so disgusted that I psychologically detached myself from Bryn Mawr and decided to read on my own and take my exams when I had to—which I did. I read Spinoza, Montaigne, Marcus Aurelius—the ethical, stoical philosophers—looking for the essence of reality and a rationale to lessen the dependence on material possessions.

*I can pierce with the sharp eyes of intuition to the essences.
Inward and ever inward I am progressing, gaining that power
which is life. As I become stronger in this kind of knowledge,
my awareness of God increases. By feeling my own essence,
I feel closer to God. To be at one with Him is uniquely to
be myself. It seems to me that external possessions and
attributes are worthwhile insofar as they are concrete representations of the intangible growth of our true powers.*

I studied the early Greeks—Herodotus and Homer—and the
pre-Socratic philosophers, each seeking ultimate reality, in flux, in
permanence, in fire, in air, in atoms, in numbers. My difficulty was
that I didn't find any way to get to the ultimate reality, no method
to *connect* that ultimate reality with the personal need for purpose.
This hunger for purpose was experienced, not abstractly, but as a
deep, gut-level desire for some state of being that I sensed existed
in the future—a knot of anxiety at the pit of my stomach ached just
thinking about it. I sensed there would be a total effort of humanity, related to the feeling of oneness with the universe, and connected with something that I, an individual, could do. *That*
combination I didn't find in the books I was reading, which was a
shock; I had somehow assumed everything I needed to know was
already written.

I was subtly disconnecting from the family I loved so deeply.
None of them was going to work with me for that purpose; none
felt the same need, and I no longer felt "at home" in Scarsdale. My
father and brother thought something was wrong with me, that I
was neurotic, trying to compensate for some worldly lack by my
continued study of philosophy and need for purpose. My brother,
who was at Princeton, popular, a good tennis player, effortlessly
bright and easygoing, tried to get me to go out more.

"Barbara, you're overdoing this," he told me one day. I was
seated on a couch in Scarsdale, surrounded by books piled high on
all sides.

He thought I was extreme. In fact, I *was* extreme in my need—

I was starving. No one recognized that the need for meaning was primary. My culture simply didn't accord that need as real.

Then I met a man in Philadelphia on one of those awful blind dates—at the zoo—a tall, virile, Gatsby type: Stanley Reese. While all the other young men drove beat-up jalopies, he had a slick, blue Buick, bought with money he had earned. His ambition was to be wealthy and powerful.

He called me the next day, and said, "I'm coming to take you out tonight."

"I beg your pardon!" I had to smile. "I don't want to go out with you."

"Yes, you do," he insisted, and started laughing. "I'm irresistible!"

I was soon disgusted by his arrogance, and told my roommate that I would never go out with him. However, he arrived that evening elegantly dressed, buzzed my room, and said he was waiting. My curiosity prevailed and I went out with him after all. He tried every trick possible in the car to get me to kiss him, and finally succeeded—awakening in me, really against my will, a powerful sexual attraction. He repulsed but dominated me.

Almost instantly he fell in love with me. To him I represented a symbol of my father's success, his mythic dream of a princess to be won by the knight, rather than a real person, all of which made my philosophical quest seem naive and unrealistic. Before long he announced that he would marry me and with my love would become even wealthier than my father. God help me!

"Stanley," I argued, "you're trying to judge me by the wrong standards—and I won't let you. The life I long for is more real than material power. If happiness is derived externally, then one must be dependent on external objects. I want to be *free*. The only joy I've known is feeling creative and connected to the universe by something I *do* or *think*. If you deny the reality of that joy, you deny me."

He fluttered his fingers, making fun of me as though I were a butterfly. I lacked the language to express my own reality, and it made me furious!

I was at a deep impasse. When I travelled home on the train from Bryn Mawr for Christmas in 1948 I had a terrible, aching emptiness. A weight, like gravity, pulled my innards down. Nothing I had found satisfied the hunger—having material well-being, having the love of my family, becoming an Episcopalian, winning everything easily, achieving magna cum laude at Bryn Mawr, having the love of a powerfully attractive man—nothing. As I experienced each of these situations, I became detached from them. The hunger for meaning and individual purpose grew.

It was the Christmas of my sophomore year and I was just nineteen. My family was once again involved with the toys. There was the usual excitement and happiness, but I felt an uncontrollable, inexplicable misery in the midst of this love, this pleasant environment. I went upstairs and wrote in my journal:

> *It's Christmas but I feel none of the mystery, the peace, or the warmth. All the beautiful feelings that come to one on Christ's birthday shun me. Instead I'm tortured with doubts, fears, and unhappiness. There's a constant pull in the middle of my stomach. I'm torturing myself to death. The cause is evident. In my own eyes I've achieved nothing, yet those same eyes have visions of untold glory. There's a key to my desires, which I hold but can't use. I must either lower my ideals or achieve them. I'm like a magnet feeling the attracting force of another magnet, yet held apart.*

I truly felt a direct pull at my solar plexus—a real force. I could neither see it, nor describe it, but it was there, and I *felt* it.

The atmosphere at Bryn Mawr continued to depress me. At Rhodes Hall, where I lived, girls stayed up late playing bridge, drinking coffee, eating candy, getting fat, looking pale. An aroma of perspiration mixed with the stale cigarette smoke in the large

room. I could hardly bear to enter, yet felt sorry not to be part of
their lives, their companionship. I never was able to feel natural in
the all-female social life, any more than I did with the superficial
conquest and sexuality of the dating life.

---

*I'm sick to death of
floundering about.*

By the end of my sophomore year, I realized that more time at
Bryn Mawr wasn't going to produce greater awareness of purpose
or nourishment for my hunger. So I applied for my junior year
abroad to Sweetbriar, and was accepted.

In the late summer of 1949 I went abroad, and Stanley followed. The girls were assigned to Reid Hall, the American wom-
en's dormitory in Paris. It was terrible—American girls trying to
talk French with each other! I quickly decided to move out, even
though I momentarily lost my junior-year credits. Through an ad
in the *Herald Tribune,* I found a wonderful family, the Charles
Merciers. Cultivated, kindly, they were relatives of the Cardinal
Mercier of Belgium. I moved into their home and was given a small
room on the fourth floor at 94 Av. de Roule, in Neuilly, a suburb
of Paris.

I attended classes at the Sorbonne and at the École des Sciences Politiques, where they educate for the diplomatic service.
The students' knowledge was so superior to mine that I felt like a
six-year-old child. They had absorbed their history, music, and arts
since childhood; their culture seemed part of their being. Moreover, some of them had gone through the "Sci-Po" several times,
because there weren't enough openings in French society for people of their level of expertise, and they were forced to repeat
themselves while waiting for an opening. The brilliant potential of
the European young was trapped in the mansions of the past.

In the great salon-like classrooms of the Sorbonne, the professors were also repeating themselves. I took a course with a famous professor who had given the same course on French history at the Sorbonne for at least twenty years. Complete outlines of his lectures and exams were available. I decided to read the lectures; there was no point being there.

If I had had an academic purpose, I could have learned a great deal about French literature and culture. But my purpose was to look for meaning, not only for myself, but for life on earth.

I was very disappointed. Here I was in Paris—in the most romantic place in the world—and I was reading in my room and going to the movies with Stanley. Why wasn't something *great* happening to me? I felt this pounding, inner excitement and expectation. I feared growing old. "Oh, God," I wrote in my journal one spring night, "what if I feel this way when I'm forty. What will there be for me to do—bake bread? No! Never!" Yet, I was actually failing to experience much life at all.

I was attracted to Gide, Rimbaud, and Valery, who were trying to break through rigid cultural and language patterns to find experiential reality. Since I had "failed at religion," I tried to live the philosophy of atheistic existentialism, where you assert your identity out of sheer, raw courage. You accept the "fact" that the universe is random, with no innate purpose; that life is a freak cosmic accident going against the stronger tendency toward disorder; that humans are irremediable victims of irrational forces within and without; that our science and technology are leading toward Armageddon, with no God to guide us. You face it, stare your fate in the eye, and dare to be yourself.

Clusters of Americans sat at the Café Deux Maggots, drinking absinthe, staring into space. Young men living off the G.I. Bill, students, middle-aged tourists, tried to recapture a style of life that *had been* exciting at the time of Ernest Hemingway, Scott Fitzgerald, and Gertrude Stein. But that adolescent craving for manhood was simply pathetic in postwar Paris: bullfighting, drinking, amassing vast fortunes to attract unhappy girls. The *real* frontiers, the *real* challenges to human ability, were not apparent. Many American painters were trying to imitate Matisse, Rouault, Picasso—art that described the breakup of a past image of man, but not what was breaking through. It was an environment of death.

The most important result of my year in France was the end of my adolescent search for meaning through existing forms. I reached an awareness that something was breaking down. I had read, at least superficially, through most of the philosophies of the world, looking specifically for ideas of the future. I found they were either cyclical, stoical, static, or looking backwards to a golden age or forward to collapse. Nowhere could I find any concept of the future that corresponded to the magnetic pull of hunger and attraction. I had also tried to reread the Bible and texts of the other world religions. They interested me much more, not only the book of Genesis, but others such as St. Paul:

> Behold, I show you a mystery; We shall not all sleep, but we shall all be changed, in a moment, in the twinkling of an eye, at the last trump: for the trumpet shall sound, and the dead shall be raised incorruptible, and we shall be changed.
>
> For this corruptible must put on incorruption, . . . and this mortal shall have put on immortality, then shall be brought to pass the saying that is written. Death is swallowed up in victory. O death, where is thy sting? O grave, where is thy victory?
>
> (1 Corinthians 15:51–55)

This language corresponded to the hunger, the magnet, the Tree of Life.

I was also fascinated by the Eastern concept of physical reality as *maya*—a veil of illusion to be pierced. I sensed the desire to get off the cycle of physical lives into a new state of being—a conscious union with the All. But I couldn't make the mystical leap from my present condition to the transformed existence that would be achieved after death. Not that I didn't believe it—I just couldn't experience it as a reality. I found no *way*, no *steps* to take to get from "here" to "there." Yet the hunger for meaning grew stronger.

I was up against a genuine impasse—intellectual, social, and spiritual. I was in a real metaphysical bind.

One rainy November afternoon I separated from the rest of the students. It was the only day I had lunch alone while in Paris. I happened upon a little restaurant on the Left Bank called Chez Rosalie. There were two empty places opposite each other in the crowded room. I sat in one and ordered a small beef steak and a half bottle of red wine.

In a few minutes the door opened, and a tall, young American entered. He had a large, aristocratic head, with thick, curly, dark hair, and full lips. He was gaunt, with hollows at his cheekbones. I noticed his long, thin fingers, and the veins on his hands, as he took off his duffle coat and hung it on the rack. His presence struck me like an electric shock. In a moment his eyes scanned the room and caught mine. I smiled and lowered my head, knowing he would have to sit opposite me—it was the only place.

We began to talk. I told him I was interested in the meaning of life. He fascinated me by saying he was an artist seeking the greatness of man He wanted to know what it is *now* and how an artist could portray it now. He said the last great image of man had been created in the Renaissance by Michelangelo in the sculpture of David, the great, noble, nude body of man, assured, humble, beautiful, divine. Since that time you could see a gradual disintegration of our self-image. He visualized a rapid film sequence—starting with David, through the gradual breakup into points of light in the paintings of Manet, Monet, Pissaro, through the fragmentation of the image by Picasso, the expression of anguish as in Rouault's Christ, and finally the smashing of the image in the explosion of random patterns in Jackson Pollock's wall-sized displays of splattered patterns—frantic streaks of light. But now, he said, "We need to create a new image of man commensurate with our powers to shape the future."

We talked all afternoon, as the restaurant emptied and the proprietor swept the floors around us, benignly tolerating our total absorption in each other. By the time we left, arm in arm, it was twilight. The wood fires of Paris filled the chill November air with a delicious, cozy aroma. For the first time in my life I had fallen in love.

I returned to Neuilly and announced to Madame Mercier, "I have met the man I'm going to marry: Earl Hubbard!"

"Where, dear?" she asked in French (she spoke no English).

"In this little restaurant—"

She was horrified. A French woman of a certain class simply does not just meet a person in a restaurant, and say, "I'm going to marry him." My father had been in touch with her and she felt a maternal desire to protect me from some idiocy. She asked me who his parents were. I had no idea—I hadn't thought to ask. He had no idea who my parents were. I had told him my father "made toys"; he had thought I meant by hand, in an attic. It simply didn't matter to either of us. But this American way of behaving was appalling to Madame Mercier.

Earl was the first man I had met who had a purpose comparable to mine. However, I was still entangled in my relationship with Stanley. He was powerfully possessive and it was difficult to break the ties. Earl and I had made a date to go to a Christmas Eve party with some of his American friends. He was a graduate of Amherst College, had been in the air force during the war, and was now writing, painting, and living in a tiny room in the Hotel des Ecoles on a small income that came from stocks his father had given him. I had to make a decision between the possessive, dominating Stanley and Earl, who shared a purpose with me.

Stanley and I had a painful argument.

"Barbara," he pleaded, "this will destroy my life. I'll have to leave. I can't stand to have you go out with anyone else."

I was terribly torn between my hunger and my loyalty to him. Even given the desperate need for meaningful contact, I placed loyalty to the past over desire for the new. I gave in. Sitting on Stanley's bed, with his arms around me, I called Earl and said I couldn't go with him on Christmas Eve.

Earl was deeply hurt. His voice broke. "I don't want to hear from you again until you know you need me; when you know that, call me."

I didn't call him until I returned that summer to the States, after spending two weeks on the French Riviera at the Eden Rock Hotel with my family. They had come to Paris in June to pick me up.

Stanley wanted me to stay in Paris to marry him. My brother Louis, then eighteen, told him that if he loved me, he would never separate me from my family. He would trust me to go back to the United States and finish college. If we really loved each other, nothing would separate us. My brother's arguments were strong enough to give me the needed support to leave Stanley. After I said goodbye to him—we had been sitting for hours in a café—I went out into the brilliant Paris summer day alone, crying aloud and running down the streets. People stared at me. But the intense heat of the streets melted my tension. Suddenly I felt fluid like a cat in the sun, stretching my whole body in gratitude. My heart began to beat rapidly, my cheeks flushed, and an overwhelming, violent joy lifted me out of myself. "I'm free, I'm free, I'm free!" thundered in my head.

On the Riviera I hardly ate or slept. Late every night I sat with Louis and his Princeton friends, telling them of this fantastic joy. They no more understood it than they had the hunger. I arose each morning at dawn to lie alone on the hot, sunbaked rocks.

Elizabeth Taylor was also staying at Eden Rock. I'll never forget the day she first climbed the jutting rock that served as a raft in the Mediterranean Sea. Her hair was wet and her bathing suit clung to her voluptuous body. Men everywhere swam in droves from all nearby waters to that rock. I swam, too, to look at her. Nature had outdone itself; the violet eyes and perfect skin were a glory. I loved her for that beauty and wanted to talk to her—to see if such a magnetic beauty felt the hunger. She had just married Nicky Hilton, the hotel heir, and the only other time I saw her was sitting forlornly alone in the lobby of the Monte Carlo gambling casino—too young to be allowed inside where husband Nicky was gambling. I wondered how our lives would compare, since we were the same age.

During those short two weeks I was sublimely happy, through no act of will, effortlessly connected to the whole universe, free— free from Stanley, free from any man's domination.

But, strangely, while I was still in Eden Rock, I wrote to Earl, saying, "I'm coming home." I knew what that meant. I wouldn't write to him unless I felt I needed him. I wrote just as I had done other things before—without much of a critical analysis or decision-making process. I merely wanted to be with him and intuitively felt that the purpose he espoused was related to my own.

I returned with my family and met Earl at the Waldorf, Room 2745, where my father kept a suite. He walked in and looked to me like a Greek God. He never asked me to marry him; it was just taken for granted that I would. I wanted to leave Bryn Mawr immediately, and not finish my senior year. But my father insisted I had gone this far and had to get the degree.

"Barbara," he said, "you're one hundred percent wrong." I was sitting at the Scarsdale swimming pool, and he was eating orange slices after his daily jog, a bandana tied around his forehead to keep the sweat out of his eyes. "You know nothing about the world. You talk in glittering generalities, because you've never had to do a real day's work in your life. It's ridiculous to leave college your senior year."

"Dad," I argued, "*you* don't understand *my* world. They're not educating me at Bryn Mawr for what I need to learn. The diploma's a worthless piece of paper. I'm going to have to educate myself."

But I decided to do both: get married and finish college. For me formal education was so easy I really could do it with a modicum of attention.

My wedding was held in New York City at St. Thomas Cathedral on January 3, 1951, followed by a celebrity-filled reception at the Waldorf. The terrible thing was that I really didn't want to get married. I was walking down the aisle on my father's arm with this voice ringing in my ear: "Don't get married, don't get married. *I don't want you* to get married." I couldn't stop. The scene froze in my memory like the instant before an accident—the smiling faces, my father's embarrassed grin, the unavoidable, flower-bedecked altar of matrimony toward which I marched.

From the moment the minister proclaimed the words, "You are now pronounced man and wife," I knew I was trapped in a relationship that was wrong for me—not trapped with Earl, but in a socially enforced relationship that I didn't believe in. I wanted to be Barbara Marx, not Mrs. Earl Hubbard. But I didn't have the strength to struggle against it, and it never occurred to me to live with him without marrying him.

I wrote in my journal eleven days after my wedding:

> *Wrapped in bright, red paper with a big, yellow bow, I'm married, in a room with my husband, a cup of straight tea, Edith Piaff on record, the end of me alone, excited by my shadow. The sun is at full noon; the beautiful black shadow has snapped up. Together we look out—not at each other. The end of an invigorating romance. We must keep the sun straight overhead.*

> *Every once in a while I realize that my life is at stake—my own growing, exciting, creative life. I'm sick to death of floundering about. I'm not in competition with Earl, but his creativeness is a constant reminder of my own death. His talent and fluency tighten up my own rather sticky abilities. I need warmth to make them melt. His heat is hotter than mine and so holds me in. Or perhaps I need the cold to make me feel my own warmth to regain confidence. Without that, the best of abilities retire, much less my lukewarm genius. I can't afford to let it slip away any longer. If I write every night, it helps.*

2

I became pregnant, finished Bryn Mawr, and graduated cum laude in political science.

My first reaction to pregnancy was shock. I had thought, once finished with Bryn Mawr, Earl and I would travel—I'd be able to find the life I craved. But Earl persuaded me we'd have to buy a home, because, after all, I *was* pregnant.

I didn't want a diploma, I didn't want a baby, I didn't want to be married, and I didn't want a home—how did all this happen?

---

*I got deeper and deeper
into the material world.*

I realize now how deeply the current cultural patterns were ingrained in me. I was an innate seeker, not an innate rebel, so I

Confusion

didn't think to cast off the social patterns the men in my life imposed on me. It wasn't their fault either; they weren't conscious of constraining me.

The hunger became confused. I had decided to marry Earl for the sake of that hunger, but the personal aspects of our relationship were beginning to take over. When I got pregnant, I was bound by marriage and therefore felt required to make my husband happy, to do what he wanted. Furthermore, I was supposed to make myself happy—and he was supposed to make me happy! My hunger was soon in a state of complete disarray—I had lost my compass. Of course, everyone else had the answer: "Well, once you have that baby and your own home, you'll get over this need." Unfortunately, I didn't know how to protest, or what to suggest. There was clearly nothing for me in Paris or New York or Scarsdale or in any particular art or philosophical movement I had discovered.

Earl, on the other hand, was exuberant with hope and a sense of his own role in making history. He often spoke to me in Churchill-like phrases: "Barbara, this is America's time on the stage of history. This is our indelible moment. Egypt, Greece, Rome, Europe, have made great contributions. But Europe is not the audience—that's why we can't go back and live in Paris." I was uplifted, but wondered how I could be part of this.

Then he wanted to move to Maine, to be as far away from the current society as possible. Even I had the strength to say no to that: "Earl, I've got to be near New York, to have some fun."

The sociable, witty, philosophical young man I knew in Paris, who painted Dufy-like paintings of French scenes as gifts for his friends, who conversed for hours in cafés, suddenly changed upon marriage to me. He became intense, isolationistic, craving affirmation of his work. When I first met him he had been very attracted by some of the French painters, especially Matisse and Rouault, but in studying them he concluded there was no feeling of greatness, no direction. He decided the new image had to be created by *him*; I agreed that *someone* had to create *something* new, because it couldn't be found. He likened himself to Robert Frost and Frank Lloyd Wright, living on the soil of this fertile land to produce a new vision of man.

I still accepted the positive aspects of existentialism—that the purpose of anyone's life is to affirm existence and become one's own authority. It was a painful effort. Being a positive person, it meant that I could *not* become desolate, that I must be able to find joy in every minute by affirming myself and my family. So I decided, wherever we lived, even though I didn't want to be cut off from Paris and New York, I was willing to accept it in a pioneer fashion, to affirm life by the sheer power of self-authorization. I was trying to look at everything from the perspective of its own being.

We could have lived anywhere—a castle in Spain, Paris, New York; instead we chose Lime Rock, Connecticut. It wasn't *too* far from New York, and Alfred Korzybski lived there. His seminal work, *Science and Sanity*, interested Earl, and Earl wanted to meet him.

Korzybski's central idea is the "consciousness of abstracting." Our nervous systems are abstracting what *appear* to be tangible objects but are really nonverbal "events" beyond the reach of our sensory system. The word we name some "thing" we see is not "it"—the word is *not* the thing.

On our honeymoon Earl hung Korzybski's three-dimensional mobile from the ceiling to remind us never to say that something "is" such and such. I almost gave up talking.

We drove to Lime Rock to see Korzybski in March 1951, while I was still finishing my senior year in college. We discovered that Korzybski had recently died, and there was a real estate agent's sign across the street. The weather was chill and dark, no sign of spring. On the spur of the moment we asked the agent Edith Stone to show us some houses. At the end of the day we found a small, red, barn-like studio, overgrown with vines, on a hill on White Hollow Road. It had belonged to an artist and was more unusual than any other house in the price range we had chosen.

We were going to live on Earl's income, rather than use mine, because he felt a man should support a woman—which was a bit ludicrous since his income came from what his father had given him, just as mine did. Earl had been very distressed when he discovered my father didn't make toys "in an attic" but that he was a millionaire and I, on a modest scale, an heiress.

"Earl," I said, "what am I going to do with the money? Don't you have enough self-confidence to feel your relationship with me doesn't depend on your being the breadwinner?"

But he wouldn't accept my money, so we bought the least expensive house we could find. It consisted of one big room with a giant fireplace, a small, decaying kitchen, and a tiny run-down bathroom, with a built-in bed next to it.

I went back to Bryn Mawr to finish college. My friends asked me about *my* house. I was the first girl to get married or pregnant in our class. I tried to sound enthusiastic about it—the charming vines, the fireplace—but I couldn't.

We were living then near Bryn Mawr in Haverford. Each morning I left Earl reading Korzybski, and I drove to college with my brown-bag lunch of celery sticks and hard-boiled eggs. Then I came home to the little apartment where I started cooking horrible dinners of hamburgers and stuffed celery. (Eventually I got much better and now love to cook.)

I had problems with the pregnancy. The baby was low in the womb. At college one day I began to bleed, was rushed to the doctor, and was told I must return to Scarsdale for complete rest, and take my final exams there, or I might lose the baby. So we returned to Scarsdale until I gave birth to a beautiful baby: Suzanne. This was the only birth during which I wasn't conscious; the New York doctor believed in induced delivery. One July evening Earl drove me to the hospital. The next morning I was given a drug to start contractions and one to make me "forget" the pain. Only with my other pregnancies did I realize what a terrible deprivation it is not to be conscious at the birth of your babies.

When I saw her, with Earl's face, of course I loved her. We drove back to Lime Rock with Suzanne in a basket in Earl's old Plymouth, and with a French poodle called Zipper, named after Korzybski. The house wasn't ready, and the first thing I did was sit in a corner behind a screen to nurse Suzanne, while a workman put in the windows.

I entered a period of trying to make a home for my daughter and husband. It became perfectly obvious that, much as I didn't *want* to, I would *have* to concern myself with stoves, dryers, washing machines, and refrigerators—to make choices about these things. I had thought I was getting out of the material world when I married a man of high purpose, but because I had a baby and because it was Earl's desire, I got deeper and deeper into it. I hated it, but kept saying: "Well, you can always leave it," but I didn't see what else to aim toward.

> This morning I burst into tears when Suzanne's chopped
> carrots fell to the floor along with her bacon and mashed
> banana. I hadn't done the dishes last night and faced a
> greasy kitchen, a cluttered living room, and a messy nursery
> when I awoke. I didn't want to get out of bed to begin
> two hours of cleaning and cooking. I felt terribly sorry for
> myself. Here you are, twenty-two years old, and how are

> you using what you have? Earl appears satisfied to do his work, care for the land, etc. But what's your work?
>
> He seems to see nothing sorrowful in my grubbing around in the kitchen. He has repeatedly expressed an aversion to women who are active outside the home. I hate to admit I'm bored. It seems an admission of stupidity. But I can't put down the all-encompassing surges of boredom. I wake in the morning with a quick kick of excitement, then poof! I say, what are you going to do today? Make breakfast, straighten the house, take a walk, play the piano (badly), make lunch, clean up, take a walk, pull out some weeds, lie in the sun, write in my journal, play with Suzanne, practice the piano some more, bathe and feed Suzanne, make dinner, clean up, read, listen to the radio or Eisenhower, take a desultory look at the stars, then go to sleep.

In the Lime Rock area, there was a group of young adults somewhat like ourselves, with "good" educations and some independent income, who had decided to try to live a new way of life—noncompetitive, beautiful—and to raise their children outside the "rat race."

Everyone I knew was having four and five babies (Margaret Mead later called it the "retreat into fecundity"). The women were hooking rugs, cooking, and planting gardens. The men were working outdoors, many of them buying cows and expensive farm equipment; others setting up country practices as doctors and lawyers. Our purpose was to lead the "good life," enjoy ourselves, and help our children grow into beautiful people.

It worked for a while—the way of life had real quality; the climate was varied and at times superb; the environment was pure—air, water, vegetation; the people were kind and good. I went through it as best I could. I worked on all the committees: League of Women Voters, Housatonic Valley Music Association, the Board of Opinions Unlimited, the Sharon Playhouse, the Connecticut Mental Health Association, the Garden Club, the Film Society, the Salisbury Welfare Association, and the Sharon Ball Committee.

People said they were "so busy" they had "no time to think." Women complained about housework. A pose of weariness fell like rancid dew on the fresh lives.

What could I give my children
if I hadn't given something to myself?

The concepts of Freud had taken hold of the American experience—any higher aspirations or growth need is rooted in failure to satisfy some basic deficiency, mainly sex. Therefore, don't aspire. It's abnormal. When my brother Louis said to me several years before, "Your desperation for a philosophy of life is a compensation for not succeeding in the world," that was a Freudian concept. He didn't know it, but he was accepting the idea that the higher drives were caused by failure or repression of the lower.

In the Lime Rock community, the local psychiatrist was a Freudian psychoanalyst—a pale, effete version. His attitude was that anyone who wanted a higher order of satisfaction was to be snickered at. At parties, when I would try to share my need to affirm the meaning of life, he would look at me cross-wise and try to figure out what was wrong with my sex life. "Nothing is wrong with my sex life!" I finally told him. "I want something greater." But he couldn't accept that.

Freud had a depressing effect. It was one of those blocks I was able to overcome many years later through the works of Abraham H. Maslow, the psychologist who founded humanistic psychology, which goes beyond Freudianism and behaviorism. In fact, he saved my sanity when I had just about given up and was ready to accept that my hunger was neurotic.

Maslow studied not mentally ill patients or captured rats, but healthy people: people at their best; people who experience life as joyful, productive, and are loving and loved—what he called *self-actualizing* people. He identified a "hierarchy of human needs"—

basic, growth, and transpersonal. If your *basic* needs for food, shelter, sex, security, and esteem aren't met, you'll have problems. But once those needs are met, you'll experience *growth* needs— natural desires that pull you from in front towards goals that appear intrinsically valuable, such as knowledge, justice, and beauty. If you don't move from deficiency to growth needs, you become mentally ill. He also discovered that each healthy person had a *chosen* work he loved to do. Further, each one experienced some connection with a higher order, whether it be called God, the universe, the Logos, or evolution. Transcendent or *transpersonal* needs were also met, usually through "peak experiences"—flashes of joy, unity, bliss, connectedness. But at that time I had never heard of Maslow, and to a Freudian, growth needs aren't natural. That's why I began to think of myself as sick, neurotic. My need for purpose simply aroused suspicion.

As each child was born, this need for purpose was accentuated in me. After Suzanne came Stephanie, Alexandra, Wade, and finally Lloyd. Even though I wasn't a good mother in the ordinary sense of the word, because of my primary hunger and restlessness, I loved them deeply and spent most of my time with them. But the more time I spent with them, the more I added their needs to my need for purpose.

Pregnancy only *seems* to solve this problem. For nine months a woman has a purpose, a significance; it's a blessed relief to have it within her. But as soon as a child is born, it's a thing apart— outside. The child requires attention, elicits love, but is never *the* answer, so a woman is left to face herself as she was before the child was born. As a mother, I wanted to give my children something other than this terrible hunger. Since I hadn't found it for myself, it lessened my courage as a mother. What could I give my children if I hadn't given something to myself? Each one of those lovely little people was driving another wedge in my heart.

Toward the end of each pregnancy, when milk started coming into my breasts, love for the coming child took over completely. For a few brief moments the hunger disappeared completely. Just before birth, during birth, and immediately afterwards, I was at

rest, at peace. In fact, I craved the first labor pain, eagerly antici-
pating the delivery, despite the pain, because birth was the only
experience I had had, except for those few moments of joyful unity
with the universe, during which I was able to overcome the hunger.

At my first meeting with Abe Maslow, about ten years later, he
made an interesting observation. He told me women were more
likely than men to become "self-actualizing"—fully functioning
people. Most men, when interviewed about their "peak" experiences, put sex and particularly orgasm at the top of their lists. He
interviewed eight "highly sexed women" (I don't know how he
knew that), asking them which experience was more intense and
fulfilling—orgasm or giving birth to a child. Every one named
birth. Certainly that's true in my case, although about four days
later it was over; I was once again taking care of a little creature
who had a need for meaning as great as my own.

Women will have a powerful, freed-up, creative energy to the
extent they have fewer children. Most young women I work with
now are deeply seeking their function in the world, something they
can do uniquely well that in some way is connected with society.
Their energy is largely absorbed in finding that life-giving link, and
they put marriage and child-bearing second. It amounts to an evolutionary change. This female energy will be applied to building
the earth, to the next step forward for life. The population crisis,
contraception, sexual liberation—all have occurred at precisely the
right moment to free some of the procreative energy that repro-
duces flesh and blood to work for the future of the *whole* human
family.

---

*The loneliness and sense of
uselessness deepened.*

Earl didn't know how to cope with me. My heart goes out to
him when I recall how difficult I was. My dissatisfaction and discontent mounted daily. I associated it with the isolation being
imposed on me in Lime Rock where I was surrounded by people

who had decided not to accept a challenge; people who purpose-fully took themselves out of the competitive world; people who had substituted no new purpose, no new growth challenge, no vocation, just more comfort and the creation of a benign way of life. The parties became awkward for me. Men became interested in other men's wives. Chronic boredom was setting in.

Earl was painting seven days a week, except for time off to break rocks to make a lawn out of the old New England field. I was deeply lonely, left alone each day, *boiling* with energy I could find no way to invest.

Every now and then my father would call and speak sharply to me. "You're putting yourself in a box! You've got to get out into the world," he would say, inviting me to this or that glamorous event—a theatre opening, a trip to Europe.

I used to cry after each call, wanting to go, yet feeling disloyal. Earl didn't want me to go, of course. My father is totally success-oriented and is scornful of any man who hasn't "made it." Much to my humiliation he would say so openly to Earl. It was unbearable. Earl had expected to become well-known—like Scott Fitzgerald—but it hadn't happened.

However, I occasionally did accept an invitation. My father was a close friend of Dwight Eisenhower, and right after he be-came president in 1952 we were invited to attend a gala occasion at Omar Bradley's house. My father had remarried and had several sons by his second wife, Idella. Each had a general as his god-father. Dad's idea was to have a family photograph taken with my half-brothers and the generals, including Generals Eisenhower, George Marshall, Omar Bradley, Bedell Smith, and Emmet "Rosie" O'Donnell. The gathering included all of those men and three little boys—the godchildren, along with the governesses, Louis, myself, and my two sisters Jacqueline and Patricia, plus Idella and Dad, Dad's brother Uncle Dave, his wife Aunt Charlene—and Earl. There was a surge of excitement that I feel whenever I'm near political power, and Eisenhower's charisma was overwhelming. The attraction was so overpoweringly great I could barely stand it. As a result, my heart sank lower and lower as we drove home that evening, and walking into that tiny, isolated cottage was so depressing I almost couldn't bear it. I felt cut off from life's energies by some mysterious disease.

I never knew what to do in the evenings in Lime Rock except read. I wanted to go out, to take a drive—anywhere. Earl said, "You'll feel better when you get a television set." I was infuriated at this—to think he understood me so little that I could be pacified by a television set. My deep need was for connectedness with people as well as with a deeper reality.

I read Thoreau's *Walden* in a desperate stand to try to affirm reality *as it is*, letting that suffice. I agreed with Thoreau that all these appurtenances of society aren't the answer. It *is* possible to get deep into reality by becoming totally immersed in nature, recognizing that you're part of it, not striving for anything worldly. I really tried not striving for anything worldly. I knew worldly power in itself wasn't viable, but I felt, on the other hand, that trying to be at one with nature wasn't valid either—it was too passive. It also seemed impossible because nature, too, was engaged in a daily struggle for life.

> *Faced with the beauty of nature, I'm always thrown into confusion. I want so badly to immerse myself in it, to become part of nature by simply being. All my thoughts seem frivolous in comparison. Yet, as I study the day more closely, I see that the glory isn't a unity but a composition of untold numbers of individuals, each, as I, striving to exist; each in mortal danger; each seeking the sunlight for the sake of its soul. Each blade of grass is as alone as I, even though, as I look across the lawn, I see a single carpet of green.*

> *I'd like to identify with the whole and forsake my individual needs. But is there a whole?*

> *All the religions and philosophies refer to this whole with which the saint can identify, reaching beyond the "veil of maya"—separateness—to a reality that's indivisible and eternal.*

> *I've never seen beyond this veil. Even on a day such as this,*
> *I see the single blades of grass, and if I find something to*
> *relate to, it's to individuals who in their singleness are, like*
> *me, alone.*

Robert Frost, the stoic, had reached the point where he could look God in the eye, and say, "I know you are not going to explain yourself to me. I know I can never understand you. I'll bear the pain nobly, and do my best." My father's commandment echoed in my ears: "Do your best."

> *I search for the courage to go on, as Frost says, "the courage*
> *in the heart to overcome the fear within the soul and go*
> *ahead of any accomplishment" (Frost, The Mask of Mercy).*
> *He's right. The fear is "eternal" because, I believe, I'll only*
> *live once. This is my moment in eternity. If I lose my*
> *chance, I've lost it forever. The gamble is absolute. The*
> *stakes are everything. The odds are millions to one. Yet, I*
> *have no choice but to do my best and pray the only prayer*
> *worth praying, "that my sacrifice be found acceptable in*
> *heaven's sight."*
>
> *There's a certain relief in my acceptance that I can only do*
> *my best, that the chances are it won't be enough, but that*
> *I'll do it anyway. Discouragement is so inevitable with odds*
> *like these that I can more or less ignore it. The courage*
> *Frost speaks of is the courage to "overcome the fear within*
> *the soul." What other way is there to overcome any fear*
> *than to face it?*

I wasn't a great poet. However, I tried to put everything around me into words—nature, the children, conversations. I was profoundly distressed by the impermanence of everything.

> *I awoke this morning. The sun was shining; the children*
> *were laughing; the birds filled the valley with song, but in*
> *my heart was a depression so deep it ached.*

I left the house quietly and went to the hill with my pen and pad to see if by writing I could dissolve the ache, to see if the ache were not that religious core of my godless self that demanded life everlasting; that core which no amount of happy children, loving husband, tender friends, could substitute for; that core which represents in me the most common, the most universal, ancient, prehistoric human possession: the spark of life, the difference between animation and inanimation, between being and not being; that vital spark at the core of my being that makes me alive and doesn't want to be put out. That was what ached— ached because, since it soon would be put out, it demanded perfection, demanded that each precious, unique moment be perfect. However, each moment was not perfect; most moments passed into the eternal garbage can of time—un- loved, wasted forever.

So I left the house quietly to face up to its demands, to write, because the word, once written, need never be de- stroyed. The deepest satisfaction I could bring to the de- manding core of my being was that I recognize it and immortalize it to the extent of my ability in everlasting words. Instead of trying to cover it up, to lose the ache in activity, I decided to try to reveal it to myself, to recognize it every day, to learn to live with it, rather than fight against it.

I tried to write a book based on my life. It was called *Each Day at Dawn* and was about mustering the courage to face the meaning- lessness. I was pregnant with my third child, Alexandra, when I sent it out. It meant survival to me—my way out of the trap of emptiness into the world. But "no one can identify with this per- son," I was told. A terrible blow. I had thought if I weren't alone in my pain, I could somehow gather strength. But evidently I was expressing it so no one could identify with me. The loneliness and sense of uselessness deepened. I was incommunicado. I felt "no exit"; the wall of meaninglessness was closing in.

*How can I trust myself when I'm always so wrong? When
the higher meaning I'm after seems not to exist at all?*

*Whatever wrongness exists in me is in so deep and down
so far that it is me, not a superficial speck of dust. If I'm
wrong, it's my very nature to be wrong. There's nothing I
can do to change who I am. I have no alternative being to
turn into; I must live it out as Barbara—then die.*

By the fall of 1957, six years after marriage, I had come to the
end of my endurance.

*I'm in a straitjacket, bound and gagged. I have two choices:
to try to struggle out of my bondage or to accept it. Whenever I glance inward, I cringe, as if I touched an open wound
with alcohol. I'm in such pain that I can hardly speak. I see
little of the world; I remember little; I can hardly repeat
what I've seen, much less evaluate and use it. I sit in a
shroud of silence, as if the pressure of the atmosphere were
pervasively crushing me, holding me in upon myself, suffocating, blinding, deafening me. I look back at the years of
young adulthood as a gradual inner immolation, a gradual
calcifying of the vital organs, until I'm inwardly stone, with
only the deceiving skin of me remaining warm. When I try
to respond, it's as if stone tried to flow. I can't. The primary
reaction of the senses reaches my brain, and there is trapped,
is calcified forever by the mysterious chemical that's petrify-
ing me. I watch it happening. Occasionally I struggle. A
moment of hope, and then I feel the oppressive weight of
inner stone and fall quiet in defeat.*

*No matter whom I'm with, Earl, my father, General Eisen-
hower, Idella, even my own children, I feel as though I were
separated from them by this invisible shroud. I feel I can't
speak. Actually I'm able to converse, but not to initiate
conversation. If they stop talking, I stop talking. I feel
panicky; I search my brain for something to say, to assert
myself, to feel alive at least, but incredibly, I can find noth-*

ing. Emptiness. Infinite void. I'm frightened. I smile and act as if this is the way I'm supposed to be—this stone woman. I have no understanding of what's happening to me. I only know that the enormity of my failure overwhelms any tiny gesture I make to rescue myself. As I write this, there's a soul-moving yearning to believe it isn't true. Putting it down outside myself is my only hope. But it's impossible to purge yourself of a cancer. Surgery is the only hope, and I'm no surgeon.

Earl, my darling Earl, offered me the strength of his magnificent confidence in me, and I've left him loving a figment of his imagination. I'm no longer the girl he loves. And he'll slowly find out that I've nothing to give, that I'm stone and he's alone, talking to and loving stone, hard, cold stone. He'll take a while to realize it and when he does, he'll find strength to bear it within himself, because he hasn't failed himself, as I've failed myself. He believes that what he's doing is valuable. Thank God for that. I believe that everything I've done is valueless. And it is—except for the children, for which I simply offered my body.

But every time I drone on in my journal about this wasted, withered person that I call myself, a voice of protest comes crashing, surging up from the depth of me, calling out, "No, no, it isn't so! You're alive and you have strength and I'll not let you die!" And I grasp at this voice to lead me out of darkness. I grasp and the hope fills me with light, lighter because of the darkness everywhere.

*The focus on self
seems a dead end for me.*

For the first time in my whole life I made a stand for life—my *own* life. I said to Earl, "We're going to New York City. I *have* to get into an environment of action." I chose New York because it was the only place I knew, and it was the center of the art and cultural world. He didn't want to go; the children didn't want to go; but I said, "I'm dying; I'm going to New York and if you want to be with me, you'll follow." It was the first time I made a decisive, selfish act, and his self-assertion collapsed in the face of it. When I became a causal factor, initiating not submitting, he became submissive. I was amazed at the power of the will. Yet, I knew if I "won" my life at the expense of his, I would destroy our relationship. I wanted to grow without destroying.

"We can go to New York," Earl said, "but what's going on there is a funeral; they're having a wake for the past image of man."

"You're right." I agreed. "But I'd rather be where there are people than rotting in Lime Rock alone."

So we went to join the funeral. Our moves were very costly in energy and money. We had four children then and needed a large apartment. Each move meant shifting furniture, decorating, concerning myself with those things I don't care about.

When we finally were settled in an apartment at 117 East 72nd Street, I got up in the morning and couldn't think of what to do. I spent several hours a day at the New York Society Library on 79th Street—reading again, this time works such as the life of St. Paul. Something had happened to him on the road to Damascus, and I longed for something like that to happen to me—something that would give me a direct signal, blind me with light, set me on the path of right action. But I heard no "voices," saw no light.

> *Here I am at my desk again, in New York instead of Lime Rock, alone in a sea of silence.*
>
> *The children are the only rafts in sight. They're always there to do something for. There's nothing I can do for myself unless I find ways of doing something for others that they really need me to do. I want to give what only "I" can give. The egoism is extreme. I don't want merely to serve. I want to give something that's uniquely mine. But give I must.*

We returned to Lime Rock for the summer. The hunger was now quite literally at a point of desperation. I was totally absorbed, taut like a sail in the sea, stranded, waiting for the slightest breeze to save me. I was, you might say, in a state of constant prayer, attuned to hear any sound, see any sign.

In the early twilight of the summer evening it was hard for me to believe that the sun wasn't going down, that instead I was turning away from it. It was also hard to believe that the light didn't go out when I couldn't see it. I had to be told that. Instinct can be very misleading. I felt no movement at all. I closed my eyes and poised my senses to sense the earth moving in space, to try to feel that I lived and moved in the universe.

No universe existed for my senses. But there was one. There was an outer one, and an inner one inside me, fabulous systems moving independently according to laws I had never made, as did the stars, and then an inner-inner universe, working in the deepest secret, entirely beyond the reach of my sensual instruments, the atomic universe, stars within stars within stars.

I stood still under the apple tree, wondering. An apple fell at my feet; the ground trembled. That small tremor I could feel, but the earth turning away from the sun I couldn't feel, nor the blood in my veins, nor the whirlings of atoms, and beyond that, there was all I could never feel, could never know. Suddenly my human limitations thrilled me with a certainty: Everything is more miraculous than I can comprehend—including myself.

After my constant reading of Vincent Van Gogh's letters I feel strongly that nothing can be achieved by this focus on self. "I would rather," said Vincent, "spend my time observing how the limbs are joined to the trunk of the body, than wondering whether or not I am an artist."

The focus on self seems a dead end for me—as does the focus on the world. If only I could bring the inner and outer worlds together, the work might live.

Back in New York, Earl's misery deepened. "I have no roots. I can't live here," he told me in real anguish.

His work was not succeeding in the soil of the New York art world, and to him his work was his life: "You are what you do." I couldn't bear to see him suffer, so I agreed to move back to the country. His relief was so great that he offered to cash in his entire fortune to buy a pied-a-terre in the city for me—and him. We put the large apartment on the market and began to look for "my place."

During our early venture to New York I had become pregnant again—my fifth pregnancy, in October 1961. Of course, I hadn't meant to get pregnant. I had just barely started my search for a new life. As with the first pregnancy, it came not only as a shock, but as a seemingly lethal barrier to the development I needed to live. If abortions had been legal, I would have had one. I went to my doctor and told him I didn't want this baby; it was going to ruin my life. He said, "That doesn't make the slightest difference; it's illegal." I thought about going to Switzerland; I'm sure there are ways if you're desperate. But one day, while in this state of mind, I took my four children to the Museum of Natural History. We were walking through the display of the human reproductive system, holding hands, and there before my eyes was an actual fetus inside a plastic model of a woman. The fetus was about three weeks old, the same age as the one inside me. It was already differentiating, with a slight outline of a human shape. I heard a little voice from within me saying, "Don't kill me." I couldn't, of course, once I heard that voice. I've heard that same voice a few other times throughout my life, usually at desperate moments when I feel something is dying or I'm going to kill something. I never again thought about having an abortion.

Since I had agreed in principle to move back to the country and it was apparent that the Lime Rock house was too small for another child, we decided to sell the studio-house and purchase a beautiful estate in nearby Lakeville, which had just come on the market. It would be wiser than building on once again. The Lakeville property was perfect, with a studio for Earl, a garage-guest house, a pool, a tennis court, and a large Georgian house with a view toward the magnificent foothills of the Berkshire mountains.

Soon I became embroiled in an orgy of materiality—settling Earl, me, and the children into our new home—while I kept experiencing the weird sensation of not belonging anywhere.

The children were a stabilizing joy, because their lives obviously required my attention. I had taken my journal with me during each birth—they used to have to stop me forcibly from writing as I was being wheeled into the delivery room—and I often glanced back to relive those moments. I had recorded the character of each child at birth, especially a key trait—response to frustration (a primary factor in later development—if you give up or become enraged easily, you'll never realize your potential). The first frustration is birth itself—how does the baby handle the strain of breathing, nursing, eliminating, coordinating?

Suzanne was born when I was under sedation, so I don't know her earliest reactions to life. But several hours later she expressed a deep intensity, as though searching for inner signals to act upon. When she first studied the Old Testament at school, she said, "I'm glad I didn't live in the days when God was boss! Why did he keep hiding behind bushes and clouds? Why didn't he come out and be seen?" She also complained that it was undignified to start as a fertilized egg. "Maybe Stephanie did," she said, "but not me!"

Stephanie, a perfectly formed, blue-eyed, dark-haired baby, was born with a strange lack—she didn't respond to being held. The others instinctively were comforted by cuddling, but Stephanie continued to scream, wide-eyed, tearless, not sensing love. As an older child, she still had trouble receiving nourishment from love and became self-deprecating. However, she eventually grew into the most openly loving child, constantly injecting the rest of us with shots of cheer, love, hugs, and kisses, flooding us with warmth.

Alexandra was born enormous—and worried, her little brows

furrowed, filled with tension. When she was three years old I can see the picture of her swinging from a willow branch, her black hair glittering like silver in the sun, defiantly asking me, "Mummy, which would you rather spend your time doing, having babies or dying?" When I told her I'd rather have babies, she said, "So would I, but I'm not going to die either!"

Wade, my first son after three girls, was born so fast I barely made it to the delivery room. I had no drugs at all. I remember screaming to the doctor: "I'm not ready, I want to escape," to which he calmly replied, "You can't escape, Barbara, there's nowhere you can go." So I decided to try to feel the pain with my whole being—and it abated almost instantly with my decision to go *with* it rather than *against* it. Wade emerged rapidly and immediately accepted the world as it was. When the breast was first offered to him he took it without hesitation and nursed contentedly to satiation every time, burping, then going right to sleep. Once when I was carrying him through a doorway, I put my hand on the back of his head to protect him, and suddenly found his baby hand on the back of *my* head, protecting me.

Lloyd was born with the need to understand. When I first offered him the breast he screwed up his little face, pursed his lips tightly, and refused the unwanted intrusion into his private world. This behavior continued for several nursing attempts. Finally, when the nipple was presented to him again, he stopped in the middle of a scowl, opened his eyes wide, and with his clenched fists splayed out like sudden stars, he bit into the nipple and nursed for dear life. It seemed that he couldn't do it at all until he "understood." Even now, he keeps everything to himself, then makes an inner decision and follows through implacably.

I reread my notes on each birth and felt something stirring inside me. Here I was in Lakeville, one husband and five children later. I knew where I was, but the question that nagged at me relentlessly was, where am I going?

3

Earl had a good gallery in New York—the Rehn—where he had one exhibition in 1960 and another in the fall of 1962. He was trying to portray the individual as incorruptible and strong. His style had developed from abstractions, to patterns, to portraits— a stoic image of the individual asserting his own right to be in total freedom. Faces and bodies of light broke out of backgrounds of earthy browns.

But the thing that was popular in New York then was "abstract expressionism"—America's contribution to the breakdown of the past image that had begun in France. So very few people came to Earl's exhibitions; they received almost no attention from the critics or the public. We were totally out of fashion.

Nourishment

I developed the first link
of that essential bridge
between a meaningless and a
meaningful life: a sense of vocation.

During Earl's second exhibition in November 1962, we visited the Museum of Modern Art to see a collection of recent acquisitions. A key moment of my liberation from the self-concentration camp occurred that day. There was a line queued for admission tickets.

"Reminds you of the Rehn, doesn't it?" I said, smiling at Earl. He grimaced. Still cheerful, I gazed at the people, somehow unprepared for what I was about to see.

There, being guarded by uniformed men, were the "recent acquisitions" of the world's greatest modern museum. Vast canvases hung empty on the walls: one, all grey; one, barely touched by some frantic, tiny wiggle, like the trail of a worm; another, so full of orange it looked empty; still another, a panel encrusted with charred, jewelish bits; then, a plastic hamburger; next, a few rocks on sticks; nearby, a medicine cabinet; finally, some nails in plaster.

I was shocked. "My God, Earl," I cried. "Where are we? In a mad house? *Who* are these people staring sheepishly at all this?"

Earl shook his head.

"We should all rise up and take those dreadful things off the walls. Not only do the artists describe the death of mind and spirit, the people *like* it. They must delight in the dying—look how the artist enjoys spitting on the corpse. It's perverted, Earl. In fact, it makes me sick. Take me out of here. This is an insane asylum, but no one knows it. And the critics said, 'Another interesting show at the—' "

"Take it easy, Barbara." Earl clutched my arm, trying to guide me out.

"I can't take it easy, Earl. Look at the people; their faces show nothing. Don't they see these artists are dancing on their graves? Well, I'm not dead; they'll not dance on my grave!"

Suddenly I was shouting—I wanted to make a scene. I even recall a guard stiffened to attention, protecting some plastic hamburger from me.

"Earl, people musn't take such insults passively. We should hurl these paintings from the walls." But no one else felt insulted. That was the worst of it.

"Someone has to say what's going on here. This is a vast death fest. The victim is humanity—and the killer is dehumanized man, who, God help us, has become the fashionable artist. They're not *commenting* on the destruction; they're *doing* it."

Earl nodded and tried to pull me along.

"And the museum is helping, guarding the grinning killers while they hack away at the victims, praising the artists for every wild and eager stroke—in the name of art. Earl, what we're up against is insane." I was trembling with anger and frustration.

"Barbara, you mustn't get so upset. It's not important."

"It *is* important, Earl, because it's everywhere."

"Barbara, these artists and their work will be forgotten in ten years. We've got to get together enough work in the meantime to hang on these walls then."

For the first time in my life, I felt it wasn't just my *own* life that was being attacked by this meaninglessness, but life in general. The powers of the modern, intellectual culture machine were being used to *affirm* meaninglessness, and make people accept it as the nature of reality.

Once again, out of the depths of my being, I heard a voice: "I will *not* accept this," but now it wasn't just for myself but for the rest of society. *We* are going to have to fight back. *We* have to find a way to put new hope into this mainstream. With that sense of attack, I began to have the directed energy to enter, in a modest way, the public world.

I developed the first link of that essential bridge between a meaningless and a meaningful life: a sense of *vocation*. I had found the thread of something unique to do—something truly *needed* by others: to act as an advocate for humanity, for the possibility of meaning, values, improvement of human behavior. For the first time, with this anger against death and this response *for* life, I felt a sense of myself, a clue to my identity.

I began to question Earl deeply about the future, and asked for his ideas on specific projects to help serve as "advocates." Thus, we began our dialogues at breakfast. His fertile mind sprouted with thoughts, and he was glad to give me ideas to pacify my desire to do something. However, at this time his energy was totally invested in his painting, while mine was still on the loose. Daily I was still taking the children to the park, reading, and writing.

Once he gave me a long lecture: "I never again want to hear that you're unhappy. I'm sick of miserable wives! Every woman I know is unhappy. None of you has been happy since World War II when you were in the factories riveting. Don't you know your job is in the home, loving your husband and taking care of your children? Don't you realize the influence you have through motherhood?"

"Earl, that may sound good in theory, but in practice, day by day, it doesn't work. It's too restricting."

So half in jest, half seriously, he challenged me to be the one woman he knew that wasn't complaining (and I rose to the demand)!

At his suggestion I asked Louis to start a small foundation—the Deerfield Foundation. The first thing I did was bring some voices of hope to the theatre—to the stage of the Poetry Center in New York, famous for presenting the great poets of modern times. Dylan Thomas, T. S. Eliot, Robert Frost—all had read there.

I commissioned Agnes Moorehead to do a dramatic reading from the journals of Wanda Landowska, the superb harpsichordist who lived in Lakeville near us, and whose journals were being edited by Robert Hawkins, a teacher at the Hotchkiss School. The reading was beautiful in Agnes Moorehead's queenly rendition. It came to life on the stage as the voice of a powerful woman who had overcome all obstacles to bring the music of Bach in its original form to the world. Agnes became a friend and excited me by asking to continue working with us.

Then I thought it would be interesting to do dramatic readings from other great journal writers—Emerson, Thoreau, Montaigne, Pascal, etc. The idea broadened as I realized that all through human history there have been "possibilists" who affirm life and "impossibilists" who deny it.

To help bring forth the reservoirs of human greatness for our age became my first calling, my *vocation*. It wasn't easy, because the contemporary cultural scene was almost totally dominated by despair. I groped for a way. I gave a little grant to help finance a series of readings of "younger poets." However, I stopped when I realized some of them carried cultural diseases, spreading the virus of hopelessness. It was like paying for the spread of a tuberculous germ.

But soon I began to feel energized, liberated from *self*-centeredness. I began to grow. As Carl Jung said: "True personality always has vocation: an irrational factor that fatefully forces a man to emancipate himself from the herd and its trodden paths. . . . *Only the man who is able consciously to affirm the power of the vocation confronting him from within becomes a personality.*"

Joy has always been my compass.

In preparation for my vocation as an advocate *for* humanity, I decided to study humanity's image of itself as it has evolved and revolved again and again, starting with the pre-Socratics. Just as I started that scan through literature, looking for the crucial self-image, John Glenn was fired into space from Cape Canaveral.

As the giant rocket rose in a blaze of pure energy, I saw it as a supreme ejaculation: man sowing his seed farther and higher than ever before.

It's a rare experience to watch a species at the precise moment of change, of evolution, most of which has been buried in the imperceptible crawl of time past.

It's interesting that many "intellectuals" don't consider the adventure into space important. They say it will never change man's condition. It's as true as saying the discovery of fire made no difference, or that rising from all fours to an erect position, or emerging from sea to land was insignificant —just another technical gimmick, "they" must have said.

Of course it will change man's condition. It will change man himself to have done this. How else are we changed than by what we do and where we do it? Anyone who remembers we were Neanderthalian 60,000 years ago can't discount change.

The concept of life as an evolutionary process has subtly taken hold of me. I don't live in a static eternity but in an evolving universe. I'm going somewhere. Being of the race of human, not animal, for the first time in history there's an opportunity to choose, at least a little, where and how.

I realized at the Museum of Modern Art that the way we see ourselves influences the way we act. If we continued to see ourselves as faceless, ugly victims, the image would become a self-fulfilling prophecy. But images are conceived by people and can be changed by people. This modern image could be transformed into a new one, if we could see the new direction of hope.

I began to work on a dramatic presentation of images and quotes called *The Chosen Image*. I traced the rise and fall of our self-concepts, picking out representative quotes and works of art in various periods. I discovered that whenever a civilization loses a positive image of its own future, it declines, just as the unity of the classical period had disintegrated, just as Christianity had suffered a breakdown of vision, just as the Inquisition had followed the Renaissance.

The breakdown of the modern self-image I saw at the museum was comparable to the breakdown of the classical image, so I set myself the task of discovering the new images and ideals that were emerging. The thinkers were easier to find than the image makers; I began to piece together the beginnings of an evolutionary philosophy.

Abraham H. Maslow provided the psychological basis in *Toward a Psychology of Being*, the book that had saved my sanity at a time when I was ready to consider myself abnormal and neurotic, because of my hunger for higher purpose. Through him I realized those high moments of joy and unity were not freakish but true health. Once I affirmed the normalcy of my hunger, I could work to fulfill it with genuine confidence.

Teilhard de Chardin provided the cosmology for the evolutionary philosophy. In his great work *The Phenomenon of Man* he traced a unifying pattern in all existence, from the original creation to the present. There's a basic attraction—he called it love—that brings particles together to form bodies of ever greater complexity: the atom, the molecule, the single cell, the multicellular organism, humans, and now humankind. At each phase of increased complexity, a synthesis occurs; a new "whole" system is formed that expresses higher consciousness, purpose, and freedom. Now, we, humanity, are in the process of forming ourselves into a synthesis, a planetary organism, one being—humankind.

Julian Huxley, Jan Smuts, Lancelot Law Whyte provided other aspects of the theme that humans are to be "agents of their own evolution," that humanity is going to have the function of cooperating consciously in its own development—as a species, as a whole system.

This thought excited and nourished the hunger. It meant that our generation had a role to play on a planetary scale: in understanding how "the system" works, in coordinating our diverse parts, in emancipating the new level of potential of all members of the body. It also indicated we were to keep going onward, because evolution is by its very nature progressive—a continual movement toward higher and higher states of being. John Glenn's flight made me realize the next physical step of evolution is to develop our capacities in the universe. We are *not* an earth-bound species.

Ever since experiencing the hunger for the first time, I expected something "new." Evolutionary thought affirmed this expectation. It's "natural" to expect a transformation. Quantum leaps are traditional. The evolutionary spiral, from the origin of the universe to earth, to cell, to animal, to human, is factual evidence that new forms emerge out of the old. This awareness confirmed my early perception that toys, that winning the student presidency at Rye Country Day School, that good grades, that "more of the same" wouldn't suffice.

I didn't know how to participate in the quantum leap from human to humanity, from earth-bound to universal, but I *knew* it was happening. Having already experienced the flashing instants of joy, the oneness with all humanity and the universe, I sensed that the physical step into space was a natural aspect of the quantum leap.

The joy I felt at the lift-off was irresistible—joy has always been my compass. All during the dark days of meaninglessness, I followed its flickering light, in faith that it was real.

The combination of the discovery of the evolutionary mode of thought, the portent inherent in John Glenn's flight, and the overwhelming dead-endedness of our contemporary life in the arts and philosophy deepened my sense of vocation. When I recognized there was something I could do for others that I needed to do for myself, I began to grow. This is the "evolutionary connection," the link between your own evolution and the evolution of the social body as a whole. The dichotomy between selfish and selfless was transcended. I was "self-actualizing," and it *felt good.* I began to be happy—awakening with that leap of expectation. My behavior was not idealistic; it was self-fulfilling.

This was an important revelation. It negated the existentialist view that I'm sufficient unto myself, that by self-affirmation and self-service, I could be a moral and useful being. That doesn't work. The self can't affirm itself; it has to realize itself through the affirmation of something beyond. For me, work—vocation—was the connection with something beyond—the "evolutionary processes." That was my psychological experience. It's not a theory. I failed at traditional religion, at existentialism, and began to succeed at evolutionary action.

> *I've found a vantage point from which to direct my life, to view the course of history and therein my own. I took a reading of history that made the future a contingency not an inevitability, and myself a formative part of a formative process. This made all the difference.*

With this excitement, I started writing letters to everyone I could think of to ask them to dramatize the evolutionary idea, or to lecture at the Poetry Center. People began saying yes. I invited directors, TV stars, actors, heads of foundations, to lunch—and they came.

Then during one of our long dialogues, Earl said, "Barbara, everything you're doing takes you away from me. Every idea I suggest works for you, but not for me. You're the joy of my life, but you're moving away from me—I can't stand it. I'm the genius, not you. Your main function is to love me."

"Earl, darling, I do, with all my heart and soul. But somehow I must find the way to work that helps us *both*. I can't suppress my desire to do something on my own; it will kill me if I do."

So I continued, and one of the people I contacted to dramatize the evolutionary ideas was Jacob Bronowski, who had written an excellent survey of ideas: *The History of the Western Intellectual Tradition*. I asked him to compose a dramatic script on the "dialogue between the possibilists and impossibilists" throughout history, concluding with a basis for modern hope. To my delight he wrote back immediately that he was interested and would stop to see me in New York on his way from England to California.

When he came to visit in the spring of 1964, the family had already moved back to Connecticut; our first apartment was being sold; the new one at 907 Fifth Avenue wasn't yet ready. I was alone at 117 East 72nd Street.

I had been memorizing my points to convince him all morning —erudite quotes from Pericles, Seneca, St. Paul, Erasmus, Luther, and the like. I was very excited—he was a brilliant man. If he could dramatize the voices of hope, people would see and everything would change!

I was naive, not realizing the weight of fatalism and pessimism in which our age was floundering. I always overestimate the rapidity with which change can occur; it's so alive in me I think the minute someone else sees it, the whole world will see it and everything will change tomorrow. I'm still that way.

When I opened the door I saw a small, lascivious, highly intelligent man. Instantly I could see what he had in mind. Here I was,
all by myself in a large apartment in New York.

"My dear, I expected a rather dotty, sixty-year-old dowager—
instead I find you!"

I was then thirty-four. I realized I could use charm for *my*
purposes, not his, and my purpose was to get him to write the
script. This was my first encounter with someone who was involved
in the evolutionary life to some degree. He was a man of brilliance
and ego. He wanted to conquer everything and everyone in sight.

But he agreed to do the script, with very little quoting from me.
All I remember saying was: "Dr. Bronowski, I think the development of humanity is threatened, and we must come to the defense—" The rest of the conversation was his, and he told me he
was on his way to the Salk Institute. "What's that?" I asked.

"This place Jonas Salk is starting—"

"*The* Jonas Salk?"

"Yes. You see, we all know something new has to occur, a new
basis for values. I'm going out there to do this for him. It'll be a
place to study the whole man, from the cell to the self-image we
create in the arts. We're going to put a scientific basis under human
values. Through learning how nature works, we're trying to learn
more about how human society works."

My hunger became exceedingly excited. It all interested me
immensely—a new basis for values! I hadn't found it in current
religion; I hadn't found it in secular society; I had begun to find it
in evolutionary thought but there was no cluster of people to work
with. I always felt alone in the bowels of "realism" in New York—
always one out of hundreds, always losing. Finding and working
with Bronowski ("Bruno")—someone related to the evolution of
humanity—was tremendously important to me. I had been looking
for an "evolutionary cluster" my whole life. When he said Jonas
Salk is creating an institute where people will gather—*people*!
Human beings together! *Together!* In touch with each other to do
this work; I'm going there—I immediately wanted to go, too. I

became more interested in this than the script. I said I wanted to know *everything* about the Salk Institute.

Bronowski sent Gerry Piel, publisher of the *Scientific American,* to see me. He was forming a society for the institute made up of laymen who wanted to discuss how to use science to create a humane future. I offered to help him.

"Gerry," I said, "the Salk Institute should create a 'Theatre of Humanity' to dramatize emerging values based on our knowledge of the evolution of life. We're becoming responsible for our own evolution—without a sense of the past and a direction for the future, no one will know what to do."

He asked me to write all this down. I had been "writing all this down" in my journal for years. This was the first group of humans I had ever met who were interested in anything I had to say. My joy was overflowing. As I rode home on the train, I let my mind relax, gazing at the summer earth, the woolly sheep adrift among the flowers, the cows standing still, almost rooted to the ground. My eyes filled with tears. *Oh, earth,* I thought. *Oh, growing things, I'm one of you now. I'm at home at last. The peace of all growing creatures is in me now.* Happiness is the best compass; it alone can point the way to go.

When I returned to Lakeville I went to my apple tree—my "thinking tree," where I had sat, day after day, year after year, looking at the clouds and the mountains, seeking a single sign of meaning. I wrote this letter to the Salk Institute:

> I realize after my brief association with a few people from the Salk Institute that its approach creates an atmosphere of hope and possibility, which is extremely precious in our society. It is the leaven that can raise the loaf. . . .

> As the *New York Times* quoted President Johnson this morning: "The most prosperous, the best housed, the best fed, the best read, the most intelligent, and the most secure generation in our history, all history, is discontent." The reason? "In our national character, one trait runs unbroken. That is the trait of putting the resources at hand

to the fullest use—to make life better tomorrow for those who follow."

The president is right. We are imprisoned by unused or misused resources. . . .

One of the necessary steps, as we discussed, is the directive idea that will liberate the resources of man. . . .

. . . new possibilities engendered by science and democracy have changed our lives. The power we possess to improve the quality of life for every man on earth has placed upon every man the moral imperative to try, the intellectual imperative to learn. As Paul converted human energy toward the salvation of souls, and Marx diverted it to secure the welfare of the working body, the evolutionary idea can unite effort toward the fulfillment of the whole human potential.

Most problems facing mankind today are profound, so general as almost to escape definition. Yet most people active in public life are confined by circumstances to cope with symptoms. There should be meetings, "evolutionary clusters" as Margaret Mead calls them, where leaders of society can meet with scientists to confront the maze of problems with general, unifying solutions, the only kind that are practical today. Everyone knows, for example, you can't solve the problems of cities by more police, more parking lots, more social workers; or the problems of a life of "leisure" with more hobbies.

Concerning a possible Theatre of Humanity: I believe that the long-range purpose of such a Theatre should be to dramatize the new concept of man which is emerging. This concept is based upon new knowledge of man and his evolution in our age. Let us begin a Theatre of Humanity.

Later I visited the Salk Institute offices in New York. A secretary informed me that Dr. Salk had seen the letter and had read it on the way to the airport one day when he was in New York. The man who had shown it to him was in the office.

"What did Dr. Salk think of it?" I asked.

The man smiled. "He took off as though he had found a kindred spirit."

"He has," I said. I already loved him.

Something is happening
and it's not just happening to me.

I was sitting at the pool in Lakeville in the sublime beauty of one hot September afternoon in 1964. The trees were dry and beginning to flame and die; the lawns simmered with visible heat waves. The cutting garden was wild with marigolds and chrysanthemums, the flowers falling all over each other in abundance. I basked in the beauty, my whole body alive with a deep expectancy. The children were splashing in the water.

It was a time when Suzanne, blond and olive-skinned, and Stephanie, fair and dark-haired, at thirteen and eleven, were passionately in love with horses, which were grazing in the field beyond the pool. Alexandra at seven and Wade at five, on the other hand, were in the snake and salamander phase. Baby snakes were found in bedroom slippers; white mice scurried through the house to escape being fed to the snakes by Alex—to "keep the balance of nature," as she told me. (I secretly helped the mice in their desperate desire not to serve nature quite in that way.) Lloyd was barely two. He had learned to walk with great caution. Whenever I caught him walking alone, he quickly sat down and pretended not to have done it. He apparently didn't want to be held accountable for giving up crawling before he fully "understood" walking.

The poolside phone rang. I picked it up and heard a voice at the other end saying, "This is Jonas Salk. Is Barbara Hubbard there?"

My heart leaped. "Yes! She is. I'm she!"

His voice was deep, resonating, laughing, lively. "I loved your letter. It was great."

"Did you really?"

"I could have written it myself—but you did it better. It's amazing. I guess you're another one who's been bitten by this desire."

"Yes, I am."

"I'd like to take you to lunch. I'll be staying with Warren Weaver in New Milford next week. I could drive by and pick you up, and we could go on to New York together."

For the next week I lived at a height of expectancy that dominated every thought. I couldn't sleep or think of anything else. The morning of his arrival I watched my clock crawl minute by minute. I was amazed to feel this way about someone I'd never met—but I knew with absolute certainty that something essential was about to happen.

By now the New England fall was in full glory. The trees were orange, red, gold, purple; the grass was glimmering emerald; the foothills of the Berkshire mountains were blue; the sky was white with heat. The smell of cut grass and flowers, the caw of the sleek black crow—everything was ineffably beautiful.

He rang the bell, and I ran downstairs, opened the door, looked at him, and promptly fell completely in love. His eyes had an instant intimacy; his smile was radiant and magnetic. The attraction was overwhelming.

He looked around the property. "This looks like the Garden of Eden. It's just like paradise here," he said.

"It is, it really is." I nodded, thinking how the beauty practically drove me out of my mind until I found something of my own to do.

We got into his rented car. Warren Weaver, chairman of the board of the Salk Institute, a distinguished, elderly man, was in the back, Jonas and I in front.

I didn't think of it then, but going out to lunch with him was really Eve stepping out of the garden. When Jonas said this is the Garden of Eden, and I said, yes, and joyfully set foot out that door, I was moving closer, taking a step toward the humble and obedient, *not* disobedient, eating of the Tree of Life. It meant learning how to become a conscious participant in the designing process of life, discovering the laws of the universe, lovingly and with humility, and learning to cooperate with "the gods"—or the process of evolution.

I stared at Jonas, my facial muscles lifted into a childish smile like those half moons children draw. He turned toward me, his glance running down my body like a hand. "Jonas, do you believe Teilhard was right about mankind uniting into one body—a new organism progressing toward an unknown future?"

Again that radiant smile. "Yes, of course, that's natural."

He touched my arm. I was electrified, intensified, animated by a power of attraction that transformed me. My very flesh and blood must have been radiating heat. He magnetized my being, as though he were a momentary personification of that great, invisible, mysterious "magnet" that had pulled at my solar plexus as a girl. I felt near the "attracting power." He embodied "evolution"—the biologist who studies how creation works: life, the cell, the gene, the building code of our minds and bodies, were his objects of interest. He had touched the branches of the Tree of Life. He yearned to know the processes of life in order to work with them *consciously*, to help guide human society toward its next step.

We let Warren Weaver off somewhere and were alone in the car. As the inner voice had raged in anger when something was dying, it now burst with joy that something new in me was living. I trusted it implicitly. I was so happy, I cried in the car, blowing my nose, pretending to have hay fever.

He took me to lunch at the Carlyle Hotel, where he usually stayed. We sat at a small table in the corner of the elegant gold and white dining room. I poured my whole life before him: "Jonas, I want to help bring forth in the arts a new image of humanity commensurate with our capacity to shape the future."

"Barbara," he said, "I need you—you and I are scooped out of the same genetic material."

"Oh, yes, that's true. Maybe that explains how I *know* I have *known* you forever."

"We're psychological mutants," he said. "Every now and then

evolution produces precisely the right type of person for the needs
of the time. You're such a person—a bearer of evolution. It's all in
you. You've got the script inside—the attraction for the future, the
desire to be responsible for the whole, your willingness to learn, to
connect separate disciplines and people. You're a bivalent bonding
mechanism. You've got hooks on both ends!"

I laughed. "Thanks for the compliment!"

He told me about his own strange journey—the great victory
of the Salk polio vaccine, the birth of an international folk hero,
the antagonism of the scientific community, and then, his dream—
a new, beautiful place for the biological sciences to share the wisdom of life with all other fields—to build a new philosophy for the
age. He bowed his head wearily. "You can't believe what I've suffered. They kill you when you try to do something new."

"You're not alone," I said, touching his hand, then pulling it
back, shocked by my desire.

"I know, but how few—over a quarter of a century of looking
and I've only found a handful. I'll introduce you to them."

"And I'll help you find more. Together we'll do it." I had to
pull myself back. I was falling off balance with the suddenness. I
craved the total union of body and vocation. "You remember that
beautiful phrase in the Bible? 'Wherever two or three are gathered
in my name, there is the Church.'" I tried to raise our tone to a
higher plane. But he looked at me in such a loving way that I knew
I could never make the separation between "higher" and "lower."

When I left him that afternoon I was almost delirious with joy.
We had vowed to work together. Unformed plans flooded through
my mind. As in the past, I was ready to trust my intuition. This
love felt good, right, moral.

> I'm unable to refrain from being exuberant and euphoric,
> unable not to expect the vital sense of the future that's in
> me and Jonas to light a flame in every heart we meet, kind-
> ling in them the thrill that I feel, of being poised at the
> brink of a new development in man, wherein the separate
> members, individuals, having longed since time immemorial

for brotherhood, will join in a new organization yet to be de-vised. Everywhere we look is chaos—from the Republican party to New York City to the Communist empire to the old ideal of the individual in isolated freedom. (Freedom does not lie in getting away but in getting together.)

My life is in an upheaval as though from the depths of my being a new mountain range were heaving itself up. It's really not "I" that is acting self-consciously, in that painful way I used to, hearing my own voice in my ears, wondering what was the purpose of living, watching myself act aim-lessly, like a private and continual Antonini film.

I tried to include Earl. My love for Jonas accelerated my desire to help Earl express his new images. To earn the right to love Jonas I wanted to commit myself more deeply to liberating the genius I recognized in Earl.

To feel needed for the action I had already chosen to under-take gave me for the first time in my life a sense of personal iden-tity. The identity problem was over from that day onward—I knew who I was. I was a member of the human species attempting to evolve consciously and become aware that we're now able to change and therefore take some responsibility for the direction of change. Of course, I didn't know clearly what the direction of change should be, but *feeling* responsible and meeting a great person—Jonas is not an ordinary man, he's an extraordinary man with great powers, a scientist-prophet—and having the example of his life and his affirmation transformed my own life.

This is an important insight, which Abraham Maslow later mentioned to me. I asked Abe what the key factor was that helped a person make the step from having basic needs met to becoming self-actualizing. Maslow said there were two prime factors: One was the capacity for "peak experiences"; the other was the example of at least one other human being who had made the step, who had crossed the great divide between basic need motivation and chosen function or self-actualization.

I wrote in my journal the Christmas of 1964, sixteen years after the miserable entry of 1948:

> *Christmas of 1964 is the best of my life, not because I've "achieved" my ideals, but because the problem of identity has disappeared. I could never again say as I did then, "in my own eyes I'm nothing," for, as all people are, I, too, am the inheritor of the evolution of the ages. In my genes are the generations. Every cell in my body identifies me with the great and terrible adventure of inanimate to animate to human and every desire of my being sets me passionately to work to further the rise of humaneness out of humanity. I am what was and what will be. If I am nothing, life is nothing; that it cannot be—and be.*
>
> *The key to my desires that I held but couldn't use was that little diagram Jonas drew for me when I asked him the difference between his institute and some other. Not ☉ but ♂ . The key to identity lies there. I identify myself with the whole universe. I had broken through the wall of self. How could I do less, since everything is related?*
>
> *But it's not a static oneness—because the universe isn't static. Everything is evolving; that impetus is in me, imperatively urging me to do likewise; there are no "ideals" to be achieved once and for all, for every consummation is the beginning of a new possibility.*
>
> *I, like the rest of nature, am a process. When the particular process that I am includes in its activity the maximum of which my nature is capable of doing, then I'm most myself —most fully identified, fulfilled, happy.*

I received a call from one of Jonas' friends—another scoop of the same genetic material—Al Rosenfeld, science editor of *Life* magazine. We immediately began a discussion as if we'd known each other all our lives—that strange phenomenon of recognition.

Over the phone I read Teilhard's description of Homo progressivus (I had it pasted over my telephone in Lakeville because it inspired me). "Al—I'm going to read you a description that sounds like us."

> A new type of man, when we consider that less than two hundred years ago the notion of an organic evolution of the World in Time had acquired neither form nor substance in the human mind. . . . this new human type will be found to be scattered more or less all over the thinking face of the globe. Some apparent attraction draws these scattered elements together and causes them to unite among themselves. You have only to take two men, in a gathering, endowed with this mysterious sense of the future. They will gravitate instinctively towards one another in the crowd; they will know one another. . . . No racial, social or religious barrier seems to be effective against this force of attraction. . . .
>
> (de Chardin, *The Future of Man*)

He laughed. "I know. I've had the feeling."

"Al, you know Jonas wanted us to meet—to link together somehow. Tell me, what do you think is the purpose of the Salk Institute?"

"I don't know, Barbara, but I think about it all the time." He was writing a book called *Genesis II—Man's Coming Control of Life*. He was contemplating the Tree of Life, surveying for us our new capacities in organ transplants, the aging process, test tube babies, cloning, etc. We shared the sense of expectancy. "I think the social seas are now comparable to the chemical seas on the early earth," he said. "They're getting 'hot.' We're disorganized. New social clusters are going to form and self-replicate, just like the first cells did. The Salk Institute might be one of those early social clusters of different kinds of people to make a new social whole."

I agreed with him. We soon met and hatched projects—none of which has yet come to fruition. But I believe one day we'll create something new together. I've learned that this attraction for creative action, if it endures, eventually bears real fruit for the future.

In subsequent years, as I became a conscious evolutionary and sought out hundreds of people, I found the flame of expectation burning in many. Now, it appears the flame is turning on not in a few, but in millions. The "type" is becoming widespread; the flame is rising to the surface of consciousness of more and more people—perhaps in response to the crisis of change on earth, an organic, natural shift. Sometimes I imagine what it would feel like to be a daffodil coming up in spring, pushing your way through rocky soil and frosted ground, pressing your little green shoot up into the light—onward, all alone, not knowing where you are going, then suddenly developing a blossom, looking around, and discovering thousands of daffodils in bloom—all nodding in surprise. Now, every day I meet people who share this attraction, whereas twenty years ago, I had never met one. Something is happening and it isn't just happening to me.

Jonas invited me to visit the Salk Institute as soon as I could. Earl was miserable. "Barbara, I'm the forgotten source. I've activated you and now I'm in the strange position of being responsible for sending away the one person who's close to me. You're going into orbit around Dr. Salk when you should be in orbit around me. You're a satellite in search of a star. I'm that star, but I'm invisible. So you've chosen a lesser star. Our relationship can't continue until I'm in the proper place, until my work is having the effect it should have."

Anger combined with sympathy and galvanized me to action. I accepted Jonas' invitation for the end of January, and began work on a new kind of book for Earl. I told him that his images and ideas belonged together and should be juxtaposed in a sort of documentary book of new images and ideas of humanity. I collected photographs of all his paintings, and typed every idea of his I had written in my journal to make the beginning of an evolutionary text. I announced to Earl that I'd take it to the Salk Institute where Jerry Hardy, the publisher of *Life*, and Al Rosenfeld would also be meeting during January. Even though Earl was deeply hurt .

that I wanted to go, he couldn't help but be fascinated as I pieced together his work in a new synthesis.

The trip was discouraging. Jonas was preoccupied, burdened with a thousand details of setting up a new organization. I wanted to work totally for the Salk Institute, but it wasn't even finished. It stood on beautiful Greek-like promontory overlooking the Pacific in the dry, clean air, an organic structure designed by Louis Kahn, rising like a new temple to the emerging capacities of humanity.

Jonas wanted to bring the finest molecular biologists from the world to the institute to do research into the basic knowledge of life; then the humanists and the artists were to follow. But he hadn't finished the buildings, and I was already designing the first play on the stage of the Theatre of Humanity. I was ahead of what could be done. Furthermore, many of the outstanding molecular biologists weren't even evolutionary personalities. They were scientists concerned with a specific aspect of nature—exclusive in their interest. Not only were the molecular scientists in general not entranced by evolutionary philosophy, many believed it was unscientific. They subscribed to the view that there's no predictable progressive patterning process in the universe, no intelligent energy at the core of the designing system, no increase of information, consciousness, and order to counteract the increase of entropy, disorder—the physical death of the universe.

The evolutionaries believe that through the love of all people as members of our own body—recognizing the oneness of humankind —we'll be able to gain an understanding of how our planetary system works, care for all our members, coordinate our functions as one body of almost infinite diversity, limit destructive growth, and move toward the next phase of human development.

At a party at Jonas' home in LaJolla in January 1965, during my first visit to this "hallowed ground," I was horrified by the attitude of some of the biologists. One even claimed that "as a scientist" he couldn't scientifically say Hitler was wrong because science doesn't enter the field of subjective values.

"It's *objective*, value free," he said.

"Can you go so far as to admit that as a scientist you must be *for* life?" I asked.

His answer was, "As a scientist, no; as a man, yes."

Others had a revulsion against the idea of individuals becoming responsible for the evolutionary process—particularly themselves. They were changing all life by discovering how the cell works, giving the power to control life to society. This responsibility is a moral burden.

I can understand their reluctance. Many nuclear physicists had entered the age of responsibility with the explosion of the nuclear bomb. Now it was the biologists' turn. Soon, in fact, we all would have to realize that the essence of evolution is that every act affects the future. Jonas knew this, of course, but not all his scientific colleagues did.

In my effort to build an evolutionary philosophy to counteract the value-free objectivity of such scientists as Jacques Monod, I read Lancelot Law Whyte's *The Next Development in Man* and found it to be a great work. It described the fact that the formative processes in nature were at work in us and we were part of that formative process. This deeply verified my intuition that I was part of the process.

I wrote him, congratulated him on his genius, and asked if he would come to the Poetry Center to speak about where we are now in evolution. He accepted. Our first meeting was overwhelming. I returned from New York with a link forged forever between me and Lancelot Whyte, and, through me, with Jonas. Lance was sixty-eight, an integrative personality born in a disintegrating society without the power to bind together a new world.

"Barbara," he asked, "how in the world did this happen to you—your sense of your role? Not even the few women before the French Revolution had such vast opportunity." We were sitting in the Edwardian room at the Plaza Hotel on a beautiful May day, looking over Central Park. "If you don't squander your energy, and if you have good judgment of people, why, my dear, it staggers me to think of what you may accomplish. How did this happen? You're not just 'facilitating' anything, not just doing good like so many others; you've selected this unifying, organic role. How did you find it? Who influenced you most?"

"My husband," I answered. "He made me aware that man had changed and that a new image was needed, that we were responsible as artists for building the image. But I think I became emotionally involved through opposition. You see, as a child, I took it for granted everyone was *for* humanity, *for* life."

"It's not true," he murmured. His face was so surprisingly unromantic, yet his eyes so lit with love for—I hesitate to say me—the attraction I felt toward the same object of his desire: a unified mankind, a loving world, transcendence.

The same flame of expectation burned in each of us and it got hotter as we got closer. We had a common cause—to spread the awareness that each person was potentially totally alive and growing within the whole universal process. Not only did we empathize with each other, but we loved the world and wanted to work together for the world. We pledged our lives to our common dream.

As more people become aware of their evolutionary capability, a community of action and joyfulness in work will occur, which we've seen occasionally, usually at a time of crisis when people work willingly together, overcoming the innate self-orientation. At such moments, we go through the barrier of self. In my relationship with Lance, there was a total empathy. I felt so encouraged and enthusiastic, so "filled with God," that I felt I could do anything.

> If I were to die tomorrow I'd have had enough of heaven on earth to last me forever. To have been completely engaged in the process of life, even for six months as I have, is to have tasted nectar and ambrosia. I haven't "succeeded." I've grown. The anxiety that gnawed away at me has been replaced by the fullness of love and joy. How? By relating to people for a purpose—or rather, relating people by means of a shared purpose.

> Robert Frost said, "My life was a risk—and I took it." Thank God, I did, too.

It felt natural to do
something totally beyond our capability.

During the fall of 1964 the Goldwater–Johnson candidacy
was in progress. I had been a registered Republican, so had Earl,
although I was never active and usually tended to sympathize with
the Democrats. The choice of Goldwater distressed me. It seemed
against the trend of history. He presented rugged individualism and
independence just at the time when the survival of the world depended on growing toward interdependence.

One September afternoon, just before I met Jonas, Earl and I
were sitting at the pool discussing the idea of forming a new party,
the Lincoln Republicans. Earl said the theme should be that "new
capacities mean new freedoms." We're moving into an interdependent age. There are new options for humanity based on our growing potentials in all fields. The second major theme was based on
Maslow's discovery that each of us has a growth potential and a
capacity to become more involved in transforming the whole
community, and, in so doing, transforming ourselves. Lincoln
Republicans would stand for new freedoms based on new capacities and on the growth potentials of individuals. The theme should
be that every person has some contribution to make to the development of the community. (When I told Jonas that everyone with
unused growth potential should be a Lincoln Republican, he teased
me laughingly: "What are you trying to do, turn us into a one-
party nation?") This concept is obvious now. Large bureaucracies
and impersonal centralized systems can't do the job unless people
become deeply involved.

I called some of my Lakeville-Lime Rock friends, including
Donald Warner, a lawyer, who was active in the Republican party,
and Donald Hewat, a man about Earl's age, who had married a
wealthy girl like myself; they had five children and were farming.

I suggested we make a list of Republicans for Johnson, to work actively against Goldwater. That's the way it started. We initiated a campaign against Goldwater in the Republican township of Salisbury. People wanted to do it. We gathered hundreds of names of supporters and published them in the *Lakeville Journal*.

I had my first taste of active involvement in politics, calling up rock-rib Republicans—townspeople, hundreds of strangers. I found myself telling each one everything—there's a new future coming; we're part of an evolutionary process; this party is going to liberate the unused potential of people; the new form of individualism is that of people working together to build the humane community. The Republican party has stood for initiative and self-reliance, but now self-reliance means the larger self. I also said the approach of ever-increasing welfare, initiated by Roosevelt in the crisis of the Depression, now administered as a matter of routine response, is outmoded and destructive to people. The Republican party could reassert its power and leadership if it would involve the people in the act of meeting the needs of the community. Each telephone call turned into a speech. I might be sitting on my bed, calling, when I'd get excited, stand up, and talk to the stranger as though I were at Madison Square Garden.

The argument was appealing. We collected so many signatures that Senator Everett Dirksen of Illinois called, and said: "Young lady, this is a terrible thing for a nice Republican to be doing. Don't you understand that we have to stand behind our party?"

I answered: "The Republican party can't stand for the past; it has to stand for the future, Senator."

Senator Dirksen held a rally at the Lakeville Grove late in October. Standing on a platform with Lake Wonomscopomac at his back at twilight, a chill wind blowing his thining hair, he held up the ad we had put together and waved it at us. "The Republican party will be defeated by this kind of division. We have to stand together. We have to have unity."

But I replied: "We will *not* unify for a wrong idea."

Of course, Goldwater was overwhelmingly defeated in Salisbury township, not because of our campaigning—he was defeated almost everywhere.

After the election two young leaders of the Republican party came to see me about what the Republican party could do next. There was no doubt it was on the wrong track as far as the American people were concerned. I suggested we form this new party—Lincoln Republicans—or try to transform the old party to this idea. "Let's make it a party open to Democrats, Independents, and Republicans—everyone with unused growth potential."

The Lodge, Scranton, Rockefeller citizens groups were in conference with the young Malinovsky who had come to see me. There was to be a convocation of modern progressive Republicans from all over the country, and he wanted to present the idea of Lincoln Republicanism to them.

Then I faced the terrible difficulty of trying to keep the local team together. Donald had promised that he would share this task with me; we would go to the state leaders and we would see either whether the Republican party would accept this direction or whether we would start a new party. He called me after a certain amount of initiative on my part, and said, "Barbara, I can't do it; it's going to take me away from my children; it's going to take me away from my cows and my wife; it's going to change my life; and I can't do it." The other Donald pulled out, too, and I was left alone. Earl would do nothing about it. He was eager to converse about it but felt his role was that of a thinker, an artist. So there I was, undertaking the task of a lifetime, which I didn't really feel was the full direction in which I should be going.

My brother Louis (then a successful businessman in New York, in oil and investments) took me to lunch at the Dorset, next to his office on Park Avenue. He exudes an aura of success recognizable to the current world. In his presence I feel like some unidentified flying object! I told him about the foray into politics.

"Barbara," he said, suddenly serious, "why don't you run for Congress? I think you've got a chance. Then you'd have something real to stand on—instead of all these intangible projects that waste your energy and time and give you nothing in return. I'll get Dan Lufkin to help. (Dan is one of the most successful young business-men in the United States.) He'll be finance chairman of your campaign."

I was tremendously tempted. It appealed deeply to my need for concrete action that could realize specific goals. Yet, I knew that politics, art, science, religion, had to be synthesized—this pull to-ward the organic unity of the world: could I even discuss it as a congresswoman? I don't know the answer—maybe I could have and should have. But I made a choice and "took the road less travelled by, and that made all the difference," as Frost said.

During the excitement of Lincoln Republicans, the group was talking about liberating the potential of people in politics. Every-one became highly enthusiastic. Someone said, "This idea is going to transform the nation." They said it could help not only the Republican party, but the world. They wanted to take it all the way to the head of the party.

Someone else said, "You could run for president." For a mo-ment, caught up in the super-reality of this enthusiasm, that little group felt it could run a candidate for president of the United States. I even had the feeling it was natural. This seemingly inap-propriate sense of naturalness has occurred to me from time to time when considering these surprising quantum leaps in action, suggesting that something great and new can happen. It felt natural to do something totally beyond our capability and the institutional realities of the time.

That was Lincoln Republicanism—another seed idea. I did learn that the political system was beginning to be ready to respond to evolutionary ideas, but I couldn't fulfill that goal at that time in that way.

During that same wonderful fall of 1964 I appeared on a tele-vision program, "Open Mind," to discuss "the arts and the founda-tions" with Huntington Hartford, the wealthy heir to the A&P stores, who had built a beautiful museum at Columbus Circle in New York—the Gallery of Modern Art. His purpose was to pre-

sent art that was *not* in the popular vein, art that affirmed meaning, beauty, dignity. He didn't like abstract expressionism, nor the
other versions of modern art promoted by the Museum of Modern
Art and most of the chic galleries. McNeill Lowery, then head of
the Ford Foundation's arts and humanities grants program, was
another participant.

I suddenly cared about my appearance. I splurged on a beautiful Balenciaga dress and had my hair done for the show. Earl
walked me to the studio. My heart was pounding with hope. I
wanted desperately to do something for Earl—to release him in the
world. We were seated around a table, the TV lights glaring. In
stature I was like a gnat beside an elephant. But because of this
evolutionary fervor, I started making mighty pronouncements:
"The Deerfield Foundation will *never* fund an artist whose work
asserts the irremediable evil of man!"

McNeill Lowery, whom I mistakenly kept calling "Mr. Ford,"
turned to me in anger. "Are you trying to play God, Mrs. Hubbard? Who are you to judge whether an artist's philosophy is right
or wrong?"

I said, "I believe it *is* my responsibility to judge what's right or
wrong. If I were the only foundation in the world, or as big as
yours, Mr. Ford, I might have this problem, but being as small as I
am, if I didn't judge I'd be reneging on my responsibilities as a
human being. I must judge it wrong to persuade people that life is
hopeless. Therefore, the Deerfield Foundation will *not* fund anything except that which can affirm life, Mr. Ford."

"My name is *not* Mr. Ford."

"Well, it might as well be," I said. Lowery is one of the "cultural valets"--a high-level professional servant, hired by the very
wealthy, to disperse funds "objectively," with no personal involvement. They tend to resent genuine evolutionary motivation—
maybe *because* it involves totality. "If your criterion is not whether
a person is right or wrong, what is it?"

"Talent," he said.

"Well, now, talent is *for* something. What if you're good at killing? What if you're creating images that make people feel insane, despairing? You can be very talented at that. I think it verges on the criminal to support it. I wouldn't suppress it, but to support it borders on being diseased yourself."

After the program, no one said anything to me. I left thinking I'd failed, downhearted.

The broadcast was aired weeks later, the Sunday before Christmas. Earl, the children, and I were sitting in my little study before our TV set. I was amazed to see myself on television. I really liked it and kept nodding my head in agreement with what I was saying, as though I were another person.

The minute the show went off the air, the phone rang. I picked it up in the study. "This is Huntington Hartford." His distinctive, aristocratic voice startled me. "Mrs. Hubbard, I liked what you just said. Would you serve on the advisory board of my museum?"

I could barely keep my voice from breaking with excitement. "Yes, of course, I'd be delighted. Your museum is the one place in New York built to show a new kind of art. Who else is on the board?"

"General Eisenhower, Salvadore Dali—and now you."

I laughed. "Oh, no! What a combination!" I thanked him and said goodbye. He told me the museum's director Carl Weinhardt would be in touch with me soon.

I turned to Earl, smiling. "Well, darling, we've got a museum!"

Suzanne was particularly excited. Coincidentally, at that time she had blossomed into an artist. She soon did a paper cut-out in brilliant colors and showed it to me, saying, "This is a portrait of you." "I" was a horse "struck by the lightning of aspiration." I was rising into the sky, magnetized by the electric flash of lightning that touched my forehead. I was surrounded by a herd of dark brown horses, grazing, not looking up. It was the *exact* feeling I had of being touched by some form of electromagnetic energy. I was thrilled with her and turned the cut-out into our Christmas card for the year. She then continued through a whole series of paper cut-out portraits of horses, describing aspiration, inspiration, striving for immortality, freedom.

This began the second phase of motherhood for me, which was much more natural than organic motherhood. My children, stimulated by our efforts, began to create artistic representations of the evolutionary way of being. Stephanie and Alexandra were soon to follow the same pattern. The girls took off when I took off. My excitement stimulated them. For all the anxiety I may have caused them as I spread my wings in the world, I also provided an example of a woman—then thirty-five—continuing to grow, faster and faster. They knew from my example that there never *need* be an end to creativity.

We had entered the jaws
of the enemy.

Immediately Earl and I began to consider what a museum dedicated to the new challenges might do. Of course, we wanted to have an exhibition of his work, also a "TV documentary arts center." The real goal, though, was to create a "museum of the future of humanity" to show the evolution of forms from atoms, cells, animals, humans, cities, to the new bodies sciences are building— our human extensions: the rockets, the bulldozers, the microscopes, the telescopes, etc. We wanted to develop the Theatre of Humanity at the lovely little theatre in the museum. We talked for days—listing ideas.

The first step was to put together an exhibition of Earl's paintings. I decided to redo the documentary book as an exhibition. There should be words next to each painting—an excerpt of text to dramatize an idea the painting seemed to symbolize. We realized there was no text for the modern age—no body of writings commonly accepted to represent our view of the nature of reality, no "story" to symbolize our struggles. Nor was there an acceptable image. There had to be a new image, and a new story.

Earl began to develop one such image. First, he gradually eliminated the body, because the "body" of man/woman no longer is in our own skin, but rather is enlarged through our extensions, our machines, that with which we move and fight and plant and build. These are the instruments of action, not the physical body. The body is becoming "the house of thought." The mind is becoming increasingly important as the creator of the instruments of action, and as the center of values, and intuitive connection with the larger processes.

As the body was disappearing in his paintings, the background was opening out toward the universe—as we had seen it during the flight of John Glenn. The background became black, the color of the universe, with the emphasis on the face, the color of starlight, a synthesis of all colors; it represented individual awareness.

"From the new perspective of space," Earl said, "humans become humankind—one body on earth, alone—so far—reaching out to make contact with another living planetary body—as we now hopefully seek voices other than our own, intelligent signals from outer space. We'll grow together as we reach out together for new life in the universe. Going out into the strangeness of the universe will make our earth 'home' and all people brothers and sisters."

After several months of work, and private meetings with Carl Weinhardt, I set up a meeting between him and Earl. Earl's rendezvous with destiny was arranged. At lunch Carl offered him a one man show at the Museum of Modern Art during the best season of the year, November 18 to December 18, 1965. Then, miracle of miracles, he went on to say the gallery would be proud to publish Earl's book as a catalog. The next day I was playing around with the title. I looked at the phrase "the challenge of freedom."

At cocktails, I asked Earl, "What do you think of *The Challenge of Freedom* as a title?"

He nodded. "It's true; the challenge *is* freedom."

"That's it! That's the title," I cried. *"The Challenge Is Freedom*: that's what your book is saying, that's what your work means. We've all got this power; we're free to shape our destiny. We've got to wake up to our new capacities. That's up to the artist, the architect of the image of man!"

I redid the book of paintings and ideas. When I read it to Earl, he said, "Barbara, it's even a challenge to me. You've made this whole thing possible. I just don't know how to tell you how much I admire what you've done."

We planned to hang the paintings in the beautiful, large exhibition room with printed quotes next to each painting, such as "The concern of man is the future of mankind. We can build for no other time. The meaning of every act lies in its effect upon the future. . . ."

As the day of the opening approached, Carl, who had been very helpful to us, became increasingly nervous and ill. Huntington Hartford was an unreliable head of a museum. His ideas were excellent, but he didn't live them in his personal life. Occasionally, I had to call on him in his lush apartment at Beekman Place. Late in the morning he'd still be in his bathrobe, his face unshaven, his eyes sunken, eating corn flakes, with one phone nestled by each ear. Sometimes he'd keep me waiting for hours while he took call after call. Once I simply got up and said I'd never speak to him again until he unplugged the phones. He did. But it was painful— they were like his defense system against having to concentrate directly on a person. He withheld funds from Carl, turned functions over arbitrarily to unknown people, etc. One morning when I arrived he had a big shiner—a black eye (I read later in the *Daily News*) from his latest girl friend in a phone booth. It really was a tragedy that a man with so much vision should succumb to an undisciplined, disorderly, childish life.

As Earl prepared the paintings, I sent out news releases, wrote the invitations, put together a mailing list, with no help from the museum. It was a real amateur effort. The next day the art critics came. They could make or break an exhibition with the stroke of a pen. We weren't permitted to meet or talk with them. I felt like the Wallendas on a tight rope above an abyss—we were on a high wire of life or death. At the opening that evening, quite a few people came, including my father, brother, sisters, and regular museum goers.

Saturday night before the reviews were to come out in Sunday's *New York Times*, I was sitting alone in my Lakeville study, writing in my journal. Earl was asleep. The phone rang; it was our friend Warren Steibel in New York, who had helped get me on "Open Mind."

"Barbara," he said, "I have very bad news. John Canaday's review is terrible." He read me one of the most vicious, humiliating pieces I've ever heard.

Canaday said it was ridiculous to assert that man was becoming responsible for his own evolution; the paintings didn't communicate the ideas; the words were presumptuous; the philosophy stupid; and the show a disaster for the Museum of Modern Art. We had entered the jaws of the enemy. We were on their territory and they killed us. Rage engulfed me. Canaday clearly had murdered us in the art world.

After a few days in the museum, talking with people, not critics, I felt differently:

> *The effect of this blow was at first a shock, but quickly we felt liberated. Walking through the forest of life, we found that one path had been momentarily closed off to us—the current art world. This negation was complemented by a new path—a positive one is being opened to us—the way of the morally and spiritually motivated.*

> *A group of nuns came into the museum; one said: "These ideas are so much like Christianity." She pointed out that Christians speak of the body of Christ. "Every person is either part of that body or potentially a part. It's so much like what you call the body of mankind."*

I had noticed this before. Earl uses the body image continually. He speaks of the awareness of our position as humankind in space, locking his fingers to symbolize us merging together into one body.

Then strange things began to happen. (This is something for all people with the hunger of Eve to remember—if you dare initiate action, hands will reach out to you, but they may not be the hands you expect.) We had looked to the scientific and intellectual worlds for sanction, but the people who responded were from the Church. I had had no contact with organized religious groups since I left the Episcopal church in Scarsdale.

Through the exhibition, we discovered there was a new Reformation stirring in the Church, an awareness of a deep sense of responsibility for the future. They had gone through radical theology, the death of God, the "secular city"; they had discarded past images of God. Some believed God was calling upon humans to mature and live the Christian life through rebuilding *this* world. We discovered among some clergymen a profound search for a renewal of "the story." What does it mean that Christ was born? What does it mean to be a Christian? There were few answers coming out of the Church; but of all the institutions of our society, they seemed at that time to be willing to ask the great questions as a matter of life and death. I was astonished at their openness.

We met Dr. Gerald Jud, director of the Division of Evangelism of the United Church of Christ. He came into the exhibition and immediately invited us to a Belief Crisis Conference, and we all met in Hillsboro, New Hampshire, the summer of 1966 in a camplike retreat.

The first night at dinner a man turned to Earl: "Can you imagine—this group represents the leadership of the United Church of Christ. Most of us have two or three degrees; we've been to the seminary; we have big churches; and we don't know what we believe. Why, if you knew as little about your work as an artist as we know about ours, imagine where you'd be!"

In my working group two ministers called themselves cynics, and the other two felt at a loss to define themselves at all. The most active ministers were in the streets, looking to Robert Kennedy and Martin Luther King as leaders.

> *The depth of the upheaval is profound. The earth upon which these men so firmly stood as ministers has slowly buckled up. A new mountain has arisen. They stand at the foot of it, ready to climb, but unprepared.*

One evening we met in a large barn-like room with a blackboard. One minister asked the others: "Think of the first thing that comes into your head when I mention the word Christ—use free association and say whatever you like. We'll write it all down."

There was silence; then from the back of the room one man said, "Cyrano de Bergerac."

The depression deepened, but curiously, I felt my faith deepen, too, surrounded by these openly seeking Christians. I told them that Bishop John Robinson wrote in *Honest to God* that whenever he watched TV debates between a Christian and a humanist, he found himself siding with the humanists. "Well," I said, "I find myself, a so-called agnostic, in the opposite position from the bishop. As a humanist, I discover myself siding with the Christian, because in Christianity there's a vision of the future in all its newness—and the humanists have only utopias that would bore us to death, literally, the day after we achieved them."

One minister had been almost casually using the phrase "man has been walking and talking with God." Earl, an absolutist of his own kind, said that man has not yet walked and talked with God, not with the whole intention of creation.

Willis Elliot, a theologian now with the New York Theological Seminary, stood up, and shouted a word I had never heard spoken: "Blasphemy! You're a heretic! We *have* walked and talked with God." It was an impasse.

I asked the ministers about transcendence, about immortality and the resurrection of Christ, what that meant in relationship to leaving the planet alive through the space program and learning how to change our bodies through understanding the DNA—the genetic code. Almost no one had thought of these questions.

Gerry Jud told me I was "the beyond in their midst." He said he had a few free pulpits and if ever I should want one, to let him know!

> *I believe, as they do, that there's an intention of creation. Evolution isn't utterly random. There's a formative pattern in the process to be discovered, a pattern man didn't choose, but that we're free to express to the extent we're aware of it. This intention, this formative force, which might be called the direction of evolution, is the transcendent in our midst. It's in us as well as everything else. It's "God's will."*

Although the Church was more responsive than other institutions, it wasn't our ground. We were always invited guests and had nowhere to stay. We weren't about to form a new church. Individuals within the political system were responsive, but the institutions of politics weren't. We were outsiders to every institution. I realized institutions weren't set up to carry forth this kind of discussion or action for the future, and I could see the Salk Institute was by no means ready for the Theatre of Humanity. Science at its very best—of which Jonas is a prime example—would take some time before it would welcome this dialogue into its bosom.

No one path seemed sufficiently strong; some synthesis was needed. After the exhibition I scanned the horizon to see which step to take, which direction to go. I entered a period of taking long walks alone every day after lunch and putting a question to the evolutionary process, or to myself, or to a force that was beyond me. I can't say exactly who I was putting the question to, but it was always the same question: What is the next step?

I asked myself the question and began to take walks around the top of Wells Hill, where I would fall into a state of total contemplation or meditation, entranced by the beauty of nature, unconscious of myself as I was walking around the path. It was as though I was on an auto-control system of some kind because I wasn't self-conscious and I had no sense of the passage of time. By the time I would complete the circle on the hill, I would have an answer to the question. Sometimes it was a simple answer; other times it was an amazing response—shaping my whole life.

I was suffering deeply because of my attraction to Jonas Salk. I realized my desire to unite totally with him in an effort to build the Salk Institute was impossible. My emotions, stimulated by the spiritual hunger, sensing nourishment, almost drove me out of my mind. To maintain my balance I had a dialogue with those wild, uncontrollable horses of desire, day after day: "I'll try to fulfill you. I know you're aiming for a deep satisfaction, but if I follow you, you'll destroy us both." I really felt there were two voices, my emotions and my self.

Then I had a remarkable dream:

> *I was in bed when I smelled smoke coming from downstairs. I got up and went to the living room. Flames flickered up between the floor and the wall at the base of the French doors. I rushed to get the fire extinguisher and put the flames out. But I heard the seething crackle of a conflagration beneath me and realized that the flames I had extinguished were but the top-most part of a huge bonfire in the cellar. I went to the cellar and my fears were confirmed by a blast of violent heat and fire. I rushed upstairs frantically to awaken Earl to tell him to put out the fire. "Hurry, before the flames reach the oil tank and destroy the house. Hurry!" But he was very calm and reassured me that it wasn't possible because the oil tank wasn't in the cellar. I was still afraid, and rushed to get the children out of the house while he went down to the cellar. Then I went back for the paintings and my journals, and finally down to the cellar with another fire extinguisher. I saw that Earl and John, our gardener, had put the fire out. Both were resting on the damp earthen floor (which our cellar in Lakeville did not have). The cellar had become a primitive dirt floor place,*

like the cellar at Lazy Day Farm where I spent my happy childhood summers.

My relief was immense. But then the fire brigade arrived and started to dig up the earth floor, saying they had to find the cause of the fire.

Sudden panic overcame me. (I had a recurring dream several years ago in which I accidentally murdered a child, and buried it in the cellar, as deep as I could, so it would never be discovered. The dream would always end just as someone was going to unearth the corpse, and I would awake with a flood of relief either that my crime had not been discovered or, when I was fully awake, that I had not in fact committed a murder.)

I watched, paralyzed with dread, as their shovels dug in the precise spot where I had, in the other dreams, buried the murdered child. One of the shovels hit something hard. My heart almost stopped beating. Earl said: "Oh, maybe they've found some toys." But I knew what it was. Relentlessly, they dug and uncovered a dark, moldy coffin. One of the men bent down to lift the lid. We looked in and gasped in horror. There lay a corpse seething with worms, a revolting mass of rot and putrefaction.

Oh, God, I thought, it's not a skeleton yet. They'll know it's not an ancient crime. They'll know it happened while I lived in this house. They'll know I murdered this child.

Then the writhing mass of worms rose slowly. The worms fell away; the flesh returned; a smooth, rosy-cheeked, brown-haired child smiled, stood, and walked out of the coffin.

She'll tell on me, I thought. She'll give me away and incriminate me. But no, she smiled gaily and took my hand. I looked at her closely. There was something very familiar about her. I racked my brain to remember—and suddenly I did: I was that child—at the age of twelve, when I had been for the first time until now, freely alive and happy. She didn't blame me for what I had done to her. She was simply happy to be free. She joined our family and we walked away together, hand in hand.

4

My love for Jonas was a constant torture. Every instant my thoughts were magnetized toward him, wanting communion. The sound of his voice on the phone made me ecstatic for days. But my love for him wasn't dependent on his for me—he's a charismatic man; women fall in love with him all the time. My love was for his potential power to understand the innate processes of nature and consciously guide them. In religious terms I loved the spark of divinity within the man—yet passionately desired the whole man.

> I must rally my own strength now, remembering that everything that rises converges. I must take all the straining tentacles of desire and twine them around each other to make a central pillar of aspiration attractive enough to draw all of myself willingly upward toward a higher union. I must convert desire to aspiration. I must be sublime—sublimated.

Epiphany

In time I learned how to discipline my emotions by using their energy to do my work—like a spiritual athlete, training that wild power to perform precise acts of concentration.

I was still always helping someone else—Jonas, Earl, Lance—which I was happy to do, but there was a feeling that I couldn't continue just to help others I considered greater than I. So I began to restudy the Gospels, looking for my next step of action. (One of the qualities of an evolutionary is that you need to invest your high energy in high action or you feel you'll be blown up by it.) I was seeking the way toward total involvement in the world.

I was also moving into a new relationship with my brother and sisters—one that was a little estranged. Louis felt my "ambitions" were inordinate—crazy! Jacqueline listened passively, but seemed to make every effort *not* to be with me. Patricia told me I tried too hard to convince others. Louis expressed irritation at my lack of "normal" interests.

One day in his office he chided me: "I know you and Earl are basically right. You want to *do* something about the eight hundred million starving Asians—and all I'm doing is making more money that I don't need. But for Christ's sake, Barbara, give it seventy-five percent of your time. Save twenty-five percent to wonder whether Aunt Tilly is well and what's the latest movie."

"Louis," I said, "Aunt Tilly bores me and I don't care about the latest movie. You've got to realize there are times for intense effort, when, if you're going to make it at all, every ounce of energy is required. Well, Earl and I are at such a stage. Later we'll be able to act more 'normal' and relaxed—maybe."

There was no doubt that my intensity was alienating some just as it was attracting others. I was reaching for a "new normalcy" in which the joyful sense of relatedness would unite those "tentacles of desire," and I could *be* natural.

*How do you tell the story
of the birth of mankind?*

One fateful afternoon in February 1966 I was taking my walk, groping, asking the question: what shall I do next? I remember this day indelibly because it set the pattern for my life. I began to think about St. Paul's phrase, "All men are members of one body." Then I thought about the Gospel writers. They had something so concrete to write about—a child was born and from that all the rest followed. Everyone could understand that birth, from peasant to priest to king. I was angry, deprived of a *reality*. The gut-level hunger couldn't be fed on abstractions; yet in our generation our "story" was so abstract.

I asked myself: what do we have to announce of comparable concreteness to the birth of the Christ-child? I walked on "auto-drive" around the hill at our home in Lakeville, lost in thought, unaware of time. Then the answer came in a flash: what we have to announce is, precisely, a birth. A new child *is* born: mankind. Our birth had been heralded by the wise men of the ages—*we are one.* But until our nervous system linked up to create a common awareness, a consciousness of ourselves as a whole, we were prenatal, growing in the womb of history. Now we're born into the universe, awakening to ourselves, seeking our role in universal affairs. The commandment was so clear: "Go tell the story of the birth of mankind!" I felt transfigured by this awareness.

In the same flash, unrelated to the passing of time, I sensed myself as part of the body of mankind, just as each cell is part of my body. I sensed the body of mankind struggling to coordinate all its functions, attempting to work together as one whole system, its members awakening to their own growth potential within the body, while the whole body of humanity was looking outward into the universe, reaching for universal action and consciousness.

In my mind's eye, or my body's eye, or wherever this was happening, I felt our birth as a dance. I wanted to dance the story of our birth, right there on the hill! I began to hear music, first a silence more profound than quietness—a full no-thing-ness; then the awesome thunder of creation, the coming together of the clouds of hydrogen atoms, the supernova—giant stars exploding into suns —the music of the galaxies, the themes of the earths, the first little cells, the animals, the early people, the uniting of people into one, the cosmic birth, the pain, the release, the joy, the opening of our eyes, the seeing of the light of a new dawn, a future in the universe, the distant approach of "other life," a flood of love. It was in vivid color, a three-dimensional, multimedia drama of our genesis. Multitudes of artists were at play in my mind, creating this fantastic story.

I felt as if I'd been in a trance. Overwhelmed with excitement, I began to run across the top of the hill, past the beautiful, bare branches etched against the pale February sky. Tears were streaming down my cheeks, nearly freezing in the bitter cold. *Finally* what I had yearned for and prayed for all those silent hours—while reading about the lives of St. Paul, St. Joan, St. Teresa, Aurobindo, railing against the forces that be that they never communicated with me—had happened. *Finally* my mind had opened to a larger reality. I had experienced the state of consciousness of total relatedness. My narrow self-awareness had dissolved and in reality I *knew* the whole body as one, and, once known, it can never be denied. I ran home from the hill, arriving at the house breathless.

Earl was painting; I decided to wait to tell him, because he was never responsive when interrupted in the studio. The children were still at school. I was alone in the house, so I went to my study, started a fire in the fireplace, and stared at the flames—still dazed.

I think the experience was stimulated, not only by the persistent searching hunger, but by my habit of putting my mind's eye into space. Ever since John Glenn's flight, I was able to get off our earth, visually. From the perspective of space I could see the whole. From earth, humanity looks incredibly complex, but from outside, we're clearly one, just as from inside your body you're composed of trillions of unique cells performing countless complex tasks, but looking at yourself in a mirror, you're one body.

Even more exciting than the oneness was the experience of the *event* of mankind's birth into the universe, our going through the transition from earth-only to universal life. It was a historical event, just like the birth of Christ. It was happening to us now, in a cosmic "twinkling of an eye," in the third quarter of the twentieth century.

I was flooded with love for the whole body of mankind, just as much as for any child at birth. It was *impossible* to love one part of the body more than the other, any more than I could love one hand and not the other. In fact, the feeling went beyond love. The obviousness of being whole, of being one of billions of members of "my" larger body, directed my love toward something beyond my larger self. I felt closer than ever to the magnetic source of attraction.

Warmed by the fire and a cup of steaming tea, I pondered the commandment: go tell the story of the birth of mankind. But how? I raised my eyes in gratitude. Thank God. I had yearned all my life to know what I was supposed to do. The message was simple enough, but the way? Tantalizing! I didn't know how to do it.

To most people mankind is still an invisible entity. Abstractly, everyone recognizes that we're related to each other. But to *know*, we have to *feel* the oneness and the birth as a personal, intimate experience. I knew it had happened to me. I wasn't insane. It's like falling in love. People can tell you it isn't real, but you know better.

How could it happen to enough others so the whole body would awaken from its "postnatal torpor" and love itself and start growing? Why wasn't it happening to others? Or was it, one by one? I had to find a way to link up with those who had already experienced the "birth." That was a clue to telling the story. It couldn't be told by one person. But how could I find them? I fell back on the only thing I knew how to do: a book.

That evening at cocktails I told Earl about the epiphany and my commandment. His response was pleased but passive: he didn't want to take any initiative away from me.

I began to organize all the materials I'd developed for *The Challenge Is Freedom*, deciding to index every idea, then piece together the story of the birth of mankind. I would work in dialogue with Earl, thinking of each question as a magnet to draw out from him yet another small but brilliant piece and place it in the dazzling whole.

An unusual relationship developed between us. He considered himself a painter; that was his arena of initiative, and he worked at it seven days a week. Mine was the hunger for meaning. He responded with insights; then I again took the initiative in directing further questions, organizing, editing, communicating to friends, finding publishers, and, at last, acting upon the vision of humanity becoming one body growing toward universal life. He was deeply appreciative of my initiative and I of his insights. We had a true, creative partnership, a union to create something unique, something as different from either of us as a child is from its parents.

I spent the entire summer of 1966 literally on the floor of my study, kneeling over hundreds of pieces of paper, each with a sep-

arate idea, since no table in the house was large enough to hold
them all at once. I could see the pieces fitting together into one
great synthesis of the multiplicity of events occurring today on
planet earth. My happiness came from seeing meaning in everything, with the expectation of sharing that meaning and connecting
with others through that act of sharing.

> *I've gained access to emotional contact with the body of
> mankind. I'm in touch. Thinking of those I love throughout
> the world, at work far away, I feel nourished and energized,
> even though they aren't in communication with me. The
> good they do is done to me, and whatever I achieve is theirs.
> I benefit from their acts as my flesh is firm because the blood-
> stream silently carries food to cells I can't see.*

> *My oppressive need to be in direct contact with certain
> people has been fulfilled by the awareness that everything I
> do touches them. To the extent I achieve the aims of my
> work, Earl, Jonas, Lance, are facilitated. And vice versa.*

> *If we are one body, then, we are one body!*

In 1964 Mademoiselle Baldet had come to stay with us as
governess to the children. Her help gave me the time I desperately
needed to work on "the story." At night, after she and the children
and Earl had gone to bed, I would return to the living room, start
the fire, turn on some Beethoven, and pace the floor for hours,
looking at Earl's paintings of people's faces as starlight against the
infinite darkness of the universe. Tears of joy filled my eyes as I
thought about the past goodness of humankind—the struggle out
of the caves, the raising of children in the deserts, the mountains,
the snows, the storms, the animals, the plagues, the pain, the diseases, the constant death, death, death. The nobility of the struggle
to survive exalted me. Then I thought of the "glory which shall be
revealed in us": the birth toward universal consciousness and action as we coordinate our internal systems and become a universal

species. It was the birth experience relived and relived until it became a normal state of consciousness.

I lived in cosmic time.

As I worked on the story I began to *feel* in my own body specific details of humanity's struggle to survive. "I" was struggling; "my" life was at stake. I sensed our electronic nervous system flashing signals of pain around our whole body. Once, for a terrible instant I felt a searing, unbearable anguish—the pain of each member of humanity: hunger; torture; cancer; paralysis; burns; automobile accidents; people in solitary confinement; soldiers with their eyes being blown out; mothers with their children dying at birth. I couldn't stand it. I was working on the floor of my study when it happened. I began to sob hysterically and ran from the house to my thinking tree, where I sat and cried and meditated. Deep inside I knew the suffering would end; it was a phase. There would be new challenges, new pains, but not these, dear God, not these: They're not necessary; they're avoidable; we're given the knowledge as mankind to enable all of us to fulfill our lives to an untold destiny. If we can coordinate ourselves as one, we can liberate each other.

I sensed the depletion of our past energy sources, the fossil fuels, and the search for new sources. I re-experienced the joy of the lift-offs into space as the personal birth experience of the body of mankind, struggling laboriously out of earth's cocoon. I felt the awakening of all members of the body to their own growth within the whole. The Civil Rights movement, the various protest liberation movements against injustice and dictatorship, were my own protest against loss of potential; the personal growth movement was the unlocking of the dormant potential in each person. I understood the shift that's occurring in the political system, the scientific system, the artistic system, the social system, as the shift from "prenatal" to "postnatal" life. People were being freed from the womb tasks for their new functions in a planetary body now requiring conscious coordination for survival.

Feeling myself as a vibrant part of the body of humankind I kept re-experiencing the cosmic birth as though a deep memory was awakened. I lived in cosmic time: "My" life span was the billions of years of creation; "my" past was the history of the birth of mankind; "I" was created at the beginning of the universe. The original hydrogen atoms that gathered together in clouds and condensed by attraction into supernovas and exploded to form the heavier elements in our sun was my formation in the womb of the universe. Those atoms are in my body now; the salt of the early seas of earth runs in my blood now; those seas flow in my veins; the minerals form my bones. I swam with the prelife forms—the large molecules floating blindly, passively, with the tides. Suddenly they—"I"—discovered how to become cells. "We" entered a cellular pattern and could see, move, feel, initiate, replicate. The information coded in the DNA of my cells includes the experience of those ancient, complex little ancestors. I lived through the development of the biosphere. We built it—we cells. Once there was no biosphere, but as the cells developed into multicellular organisms, learned to unite in a more wholistic manner, and gained solar energy from the process of photosynthesis, we began to evolve the air and vegetation that was translated into our bodies.

I lived through evolution as our history, my history. I could close my eyes at any time and see it as a rapid film sequence of an evolutionary spiral of our own birth, a movie of creation, a "photogenesis" in three-dimensional light. The background was the universe, the billions and billions of stars around which planetary systems revolve. I sensed consciousness such as our own. As I experienced ourselves coordinating and synergizing as one cosmic body, the presence of other cosmic bodies stimulated me so clearly that I felt surrounded by life. It was on the tip of my tongue to be able to communicate with it, and on the tip of its tongue to be able to communicate with me. I sensed we were not alone, that, like a newborn child, we were surrounded by life but were too immature to understand or communicate. We were going through a "viability" test. Could we learn to coordinate ourselves—or would we tear ourselves apart and not make it to the next step, an abortive, planetary dropout? As Earl put it in *The Search Is On:*

> From the dumb, dark womb of evolution, mankind has been born. Our eyes and ears are open. The universe speaks and we begin to listen and try to understand. As one body we study the new descriptions of the forces of creation gleaned for us by science, the sensory system of mankind, and in the light of our dawning awareness, we search for the intention of creation and the role we can now play in universal affairs.
>
> Our lifetime marks the birth of mankind, for we are the generation born at the time that mankind was born. We are the first generation to be aware of ourselves as one and responsible for the future of the whole.

As I worked on the book, my sense of mission grew. I entered a different state of being. I wasn't self-conscious; I was on a different time scale, not worried about anything; all fretfulness was gone; I was in a state of joy.

When I "click" into the state of empathy, of "feeling with" the whole body, I *am* it! I'm *living* the experience, not thinking about it, or telling it—I am *it*. When I am it, it has an irresistible reality. I'm not yet strong enough to stay in this state of empathy, but I've learned to enter the empathetic state of consciousness whenever any person talks to me who hungers to connect. It doesn't matter who the person is—a child, someone on a bus, a professor. I feel exactly the same with all people who experience the hunger. In this state of consciousness, there's a new awareness of equality. If the person is with you and you're wholly with that person, there's no judgment.

I was possessed by my own desire.

During my work on the book, I was in a state of joy. I would call Jonas or wait for his call; I would call Lance or wait for him to visit; then I would share the book with them.

Lance Whyte came to visit in Lakeville when I had just about finished *The Birth of Mankind*. I read portions of it to him, as we sat on the couch in my study. He got so excited he moved farther and farther forward in his seat and finally fell off.

He said it was authentic, essential, wonderful. "This is your work?" he asked.

I shook my head. "No, it's Earl's. The words came out of Earl's mouth through my questioning and probing and trying to find all the pieces. He has a powerful capacity to make images. This is really his work; I'm just editing it."

Lance became furious with me and didn't want to discuss it with Earl. I couldn't persuade him that Earl had truly said these things. I ran into the same problem with Jonas. He identified the words with me. This was painful because it wasn't fair. Earl originally said the words and the words became flesh for me. I lived and breathed and felt every minute of the day and night the birth of mankind and the excitement of the next step.

Earl was continuing to develop the image of a face, the color of starlight, against the background of black. He used me as a model. I sat for a photograph in the breakfast room, looking up to the sky, and thinking with all my being: *we are mankind, born into the universe, seeking a greater awareness of the creative intention.* He did a portrait from that photograph—a portrait of a state of consciousness, the expectation of universal life, a face the color of starlight looking outward to the infinite black of space. Some days, when working on the book, I would stare at it for hours; it helped me relive the "experience on the hill."

We were trying to symbolize the experience of expectation, the beginning of an image and a text of our cosmic genesis that might become suitable for the first universal age. In 1966 Jonas was embroiled in the struggle to create the institute, to raise funds, to handle the human conflicts that arose out of doing an utterly new thing, and I looked upon his institute as a place where this image and text might be developed. He reported to me quite often from California. But it had become clear that I couldn't work directly with him. The institute required large-scale funding that could be done only by professional fund raisers.

The scientists themselves were not attracted to the vision of evolutionary transformation. In fact, many of them were narrow-minded, ego-centered, and *against* Jonas' vision of synthesis. They argued over research grants, secretaries, paper clips! I represented something disruptive to Jonas' effort, because I found myself in philosophical argument with them. I had such a powerful drive "to tell the story of the birth of mankind" that I was no longer really trying to help someone else anyway. I began to feel that the message of the birth was as important as what he was doing.

Also, I was too attracted to work with him. He was in my thoughts every second. I had to exert continual energy *not* to call, write, or fly to him. It was like holding two powerful attracting magnets apart. This created so much tension that I made a decision, drawn from the very core of my desire for higher convergence: I vowed never, never to touch him again physically, even though I loved him passionately. It was the only way to become free. Sex is a possessive emotion and I was possessed by my own desire, its victim. I imagined that as I continued to rise toward awareness of our oneness and the ability to tell the story well, I would unite with him on a higher level. For days I practiced, literally pulling my wild thoughts away from the object of their desire, like Atlas lifting weights. Every emotional muscle strained to separate from this obsession. I succeeded a little. I could feel my emotions accepting the higher convergence, beginning to be attracted toward "it" rather than "him."

The day I finished the book I went to New York to see him. I was in a state of bliss; "having" a book was like having a baby. I had a copy of the manuscript for him, and I had made my decision about him. But I was still longing to share this joy, to thank him for the part he (unwittingly) played through his affection for me. He had done it by being himself. I was just about to tell him when he casually mentioned he had fallen in love with some woman. He went on, oblivious to my horror, seeking my sympathy at the complex situation he was in. I froze in total misery, speechless.

After a while he noticed. "What's wrong?"

The idiocy of his not even *knowing* completely devastated me. I began to cry during lunch at the Carlyle—great, loud sobs—so he took me to his room, and tried to comfort me. But I stiffened in resistance. He gave me his handkerchief.

"Jonas, I had already decided never to touch you again," I said, noticing the surprise on his face. "It just shocked my system to hear you loved someone else. Don't worry about me." I was still sobbing violently. "I'll be fine. I'll always love you, but it has nothing to do with you. It's your understanding of evolution."

I got up, stiff with grief, my legs almost buckling like fragile sticks. When I left him I was still carrying my manuscript—he hadn't even seen it.

---

*I wanted to link with others
who shared a similar experience.*

I began the laborious effort of trying to get the book published. It was like trying to get a bright but unusual child into school. The amazing difference in response to *The Birth of Mankind*—from Lance's falling off the couch to total lack of understanding—had to *mean* something. It was a signal. From the day of epiphany I wanted to link with others who shared a similar experience. I felt that the electric current that expanded my individual consciousness would become continually available if *enough* people connected and formed a group channel of receiving and communicating awareness.

In a flash of excitement I decided to start my own publication. I would find people all over the world who had the joy inside, write to them, ask their ideas about the next step for the future good, and offer to publish excerpts of their thoughts in "The Center Letter," to share with others on the same frontier. I started to list everyone I had ever heard of or read about who was interested in the future. I anticipated a quantum leap when enough people were linked with each other—people who experienced this instant communication of which Teilhard had spoken.

I wrote to Abraham Maslow, telling him his book *Toward a Psychology of Being* had saved my life. Now I wanted to identify others throughout the world so we could be in closer touch with each other. He wrote back immediately that this was essential and that he'd like to meet me. When he came to lunch at the New York apartment, I saw he was different from Jonas and Lance—tall, slim, with a moustache and a wonderful, wise, weather-beaten face. He had a deep curiosity about what made people good. He questioned me at length about *why* I was doing all this. He kept nodding. I was an example of his theory of self-actualizing people. He had a pronounced goodness, but was tough—a fighter for life.

"One thing I've learned, Barbara, is that you have to fight back. You're right not to let the bastards kill you. You can't permit those who would degrade man to prevail." He told me he wanted to start a publication called *Assent,* and he talked about the viscious destructiveness of some academic liberals. "They want to *prove* that we're rotten." He encouraged me to bring together the "good."

He offered his "Eupsychian Network"—a list of the "good people" he had collected over a lifetime, those who would form the "Good Society." Abe was very open about good and bad people. Although he affirmed the growth potential and tendency toward goodness in all people, he also stressed that people who don't start growing, once their survival needs are met, get sick. How well I knew that! Five more years of nongrowth and I would have been an embittered woman. These nongrowers were probably the people whose behavior tended to be "bad" or destructive to their own and other lives. The Eupsychian Network were people in the growth mode. Many were humanistic psychologists founding growth centers, such as Carl Rogers, Victor Frankl, Michael Murphy of Esalen, to help people move toward full health. Jonas, Al Rosenfeld, Lance Whyte also gave me names. My list soon totalled over 1,000.

In August 1967 I sent the first mimeographed letter to this mailing list, telling of my feeling that a profound change was occurring on planet earth: Homo progressivus types were spreading throughout society, in all cultures, races, nations, and backgrounds —those in whom the flame of expectation burned. I invited them to correspond with me and each other. Then I waited in excitement for their response, as though we were lovers.

Stephanie observed all this, and said, "Mummy, you're a different person from what you were. You've gone from a cave woman to the space age."

I began to sense a problem of communication with the children. They were all doing badly in school, except Lloyd who was only three. Alexandra tested in the 98th percentile in the country, but hated school and was called "disappointing."

> *I have an uneasy sense of having failed to reach my own children with this excitement I feel for participation in life. Earl and I don't attract them. We're a challenge to be avoided, not responded to. I can't really communicate with any of them, except Lloyd, who's too young to count. Earl's and my life are intensely single-minded, our concentration on our work is total. The children want our full attention. They want fun, trips, vacations, television, games, and we want to inspire them to do their best.*

> *We've been so terribly alone and isolated, working for our very lives.*

> *All you can do, Barbara, is try to express your love. Maybe as time goes on you'll have a breakthrough and be able to listen to them and receive from them instead of always telling them something.*

> *So, spirits up! Nothing is perfect, but your blessings exceed the bound. Live up to them.*

(*For weeks I've continually heard the phrase in my head,
"Dearly beloved, we are gathered together to ask the Lord's
blessing."*)

I received hundreds of letters from all over the world before
long—from well-known people like Lewis Mumford, Thomas Merton, and from unknown enthusiasts. In the second letter I chose
key excerpts from those first responses. In the third, on humanistic
psychology, I published Maslow and others from the Eupsychian
Network who had responded. People started passing the letter from
one to another. I received word from an African chief who offered
to circulate it through Africa. Someone on a bicycle was carrying it
to people in New Delhi.

Then in the fourth letter I decided to include excerpts from *The
Birth of Mankind* and to print one of Earl's paintings of mankind
as a face of awareness in the universe as the centerfold, to see if
this concept appealed to the people who liked "The Center Letter."
I had originated the letter in the asking, receptive mode; I had
created a context and hoped that through it people would be able
to piece together the new whole. But it didn't work that way. After
the fourth letter I received a long, cruel response from Lancelot
Whyte saying he was withdrawing all support for and contact with
me. He charged I had lost my integrity by putting Earl in as a
central philosopher of the age when I had said I'd seek out the best
ideas. He practically accused me of being an intellectual fraud,
which was really unfair; he always knew precisely how I felt about
Earl's work. (Perhaps he was jealous that he wasn't in the centerfold!) I wrote back affirming my intention to seek the best, and
saying that, as a friend, I didn't understand how he could possibly
deny all contact. But I never heard from him again.

This kind of reaction has hurt me throughout my involvement
in the futurist movement. When people's feelings or egos are hurt,
they still behave in a manner destructive to one another. These
pioneers are just as afflicted with ego as anyone else. It's distressing, because synergy, empathy, wholism, futurism, by their very
natures ought to help you overcome your ego.

I was deeply hurt by Lancelot Whyte's rejection, but I persisted on—determined never to react in kind. I consciously tested whether I was able *not* to reject him, and I believe I've succeeded. I love him and always will. Underneath his hurt, he must feel the same about me. I hope he's alive somewhere now—I don't know.

As "The Center Letter" progressed in popularity, real activists wrote proposing their own policies to improve the world. Each had a fragment of the whole; each put his or her own view first, downgrading the importance of the others.

I telephoned Anthony Sutich in California, who published the *Journal of Transpersonal Psychology,* asking if I could write an article for him on the relationship of the space effort to the development of human potential. Abe Maslow had given me his name, calling him a "hero." Tony is totally paralyzed from the neck down. His body, Abe said, "is turning to stone," hardening at the joints with some spreading disease. He lies immobile on a stretcher, able to raise only his head, and from that position edits magazines. *My God, what courage,* I thought, as I waited for the sound of his voice; it was only slightly blurred. We had a pleasant conversation —but he warned me that although he would like to see the article since I was a friend of Abe's and he admired "The Center Letter," he was against the space program. After receiving my article he wrote back saying he saw no relationship between the step into the universe and human growth; moreover, the space program was drawing funds away from vital programs in the development of inner awareness.

I asked Thomas Merton what he thought of the step beyond the planet in relation to religious development. He wrote back: "Frankly, Mrs. Hubbard, I never think about the space program except occasionally when I pick up a magazine in the dentist's office. I don't think it has any relationship to religious development."

Space scientists didn't respond to "The Center Letter" at all. It wasn't in the "language" of their discipline. In fact, I found no advocates who were wholistic—seeing the importance of both their position and, concurrently, the others. No one got anyone else's point!

I can't be in love with
a person who isn't in love
with universal life.

I visited Maslow several times during "The Center Letter" period at Brandeis University. He had written from his hospital bed when he thought he was dying from his first heart attack. The message was scrawled by hand on green steno paper: "When I thought I was dying, I thought of you. You represented life to me. I want to tell you to keep going, never stop. You represent life." I'll cherish his letter forever.

On a visit just before he died, I asked him what he thought about going into space in relation to the great potential of humanity, particularly in the field of transpersonal growth, the greater connection with the universe, cosmic understanding.

"Barbara, as long as you don't impose it on anyone, everyone can do what he pleases. There'll be those that want to go into space; there'll be those for whom it isn't valid, for example, myself. I can get into a state of universal consciousness through meditation; therefore, I have no personal interest in the space program, but I'm not against your being interested in it."

"Abe," I said, "it's more than my being *interested* in it—I believe it's the natural organic step if man is to become operative in the universe, the outer expression of the inner state of cosmic consciousness." He didn't disagree, it was his personality not to disagree with people. He just nodded, but didn't care.

At that time I was still seeing Jonas, too, although remaining faithful to my vow. It gave me a new sense of inner strength, this ability to say no in order to say yes to something *more* desirable. I was in self-control.

One hot summer afternoon we both had a few hours free in New York. He called and asked to come over. We relaxed on the big, white couch at 907 Fifth Avenue, sipping iced tea and watching the trees flutter in Central Park. Earl's giant portraits of the faces of starlight against the background of the universe glowed like black holes in the white walls, so concentrated as to absorb all energy.

Jonas is the opposite of Earl. Earl is angular, a minister of space. Jonas is warm, seductive, a lover of earth and flesh and life, able to make you feel as if you're the most indispensable person in the world to him—that his whole effort would collapse without you. He made everyone feel that way—secretaries, cleaning ladies, chairmen of boards—but not me anymore. However, I still loved him, and I deeply enjoyed talking with him. He has the mind of a poet, making analogies between biology and sociology, the behavior of cells and human populations. He has the same approach as Newton. Everything is meaningful. Also, I love his sense of responsibility for the whole, which, like my own, has a tendency toward exaggeration. I remember during the horror of the Kennedy assassination, he called me. We mourned for Kennedy and the human race.

"Barbara, as long as he was in the White House, I could go on with my work. But you know what I felt when he was shot? A sense of responsibility falling on my shoulders."

I empathized with this. When Kennedy was killed I cried for days and then got up, determined not to let the "torch" die.

During the afternoon I innocently brought up the subject of the aging process, mentioning how Al had told me that many scientists believed aging was a "degenerative disease" that could be overcome—*soon.* I told him how appropriate such knowledge is. "It's necessary to expand our lives if we're going to live and work on a cosmic time scale in the universe. Will your work on cancer help toward the extension of the life cycle?" I asked.

He amazed me by suddenly becoming enraged. I think it was the first time I'd felt his anger. He rose in wrath against me like a biblical prophet. "Death is essential to life!" he proclaimed. "If the individual doesn't die, the species can't go on!"

"Well," I said, "you better get out of that laboratory and take off your white jacket, because you're working to understand the cell, and its time clock for death is *not* surely inevitable. There was no scheduled death when life was a single cell; it divided to repro-

duce. Death came in with multicellular systems and sexual reproduction. They're historical events, not eternal verities." I gave *him*
a lecture for a change.

"It *is* possible that the mammalian death cycle will be changed,"
I insisted. "Extended life would be disastrous for an earth-bound
species, but we're *not* earth-bound. We can't be compared to fruit
flies. We're the only species able to leave this earth alive. Once we
learn to live in the universe beyond our mother planet, we'll be on
a cosmic time scale, not an earth time scale. We'll need increased
individual development—variety and depth of wisdom and experience, rather than reproduction of multitudes of new individuals.

"If it's true that the potential of the human mind has barely
been tapped, that unused capacity will be required for the development of our universal step. We must live longer when we leave
this earth. I don't think it's an accident that rocketry, genetics,
cybernetics, and the recognition of the limitations of our finite
globe all occurred within the same generation. It's natural!" I felt it
because of the birth experience.

He disagreed violently. He even said if he thought he were
contributing to that possibility, he'd leave the laboratory. The
strength of his anger shocked me. When he made it clear that he
wasn't in favor of the effort to become a universal species, my
physical-spiritual attraction to him personally completely disappeared, instantly, as though a light had suddenly burned out. I was
amazed that passion of that strength could disappear the second I
perceived he was against what I felt to be the next step. For me,
attraction is based on the hunger for evolution. I can't be *in* love
with a person who isn't in love with universal consciousness
through action—or universal life. The magnetism was gone. I was
left only with the memory of a great love that made me grow into a
new woman. But I continued to respect, admire, and learn from his
work, which is now focusing on the transition from the growth
phase Epoch A to the growth phase Epoch B, in which we'll learn
to limit the population growth of our species and move from competitive toward cooperative behavior.

Subsequently, I've come to feel that this newly discovered difference among human beings—whether or not they are attracted to extending their earth lives and going to space physically—is a deep psychogenetic trait that wasn't apparent until the choice of *literal* transformation and transcendence became historically available. Before, it was the "mystical leap": life after death. Now we've begun to develop the tools of transformation, moving toward the Tree of Life. We're conceiving of life after earth. The attraction doesn't depend on intellect and reason, but rather what Robert Frost called "passionate preference."

As I probed Jonas' *emotional* rejection, it turned out to be more a matter of his not *wanting* this future than rationally proving to me it was impossible. Neither of us had proof, since the step hasn't occurred yet. A while later, I had another meeting with him at the Westchester Country Club. He had been thinking about our conversation. Being a constructive man, he had a solution for me.

During our first conversation, I had said, "Jonas, you realize the sun is going to expand and destroy this earth. It's many billions of years away, but I can't recommend as a 'pro-life policy' that we just sit here and wait to be destroyed when we know we have the capability of transcending the earth. How can you say that we shouldn't if you know the earth is going to be destroyed?"

His solution to my need for life everlasting, in reality, not in metaphor, was this: "I think it'll be possible to transform the cycle of the sun so that it won't destroy the earth, so that we can stay here without being destroyed."

My heart sank. It was as though my parents had said to me when I was two years old in that crib, shaking the bars: "Dear child, you'll be able to stay in the crib forever; don't worry; you'll be taken care of; there's no need for you to get out." I felt as if he were putting a plastic bag over my head, slowly suffocating me.

"Jonas, the point is, I *want* to leave earth." I was amazed at my own words. Until pressed, I hadn't put it that way, even to myself. I reiterated. "Yes, I *love* earth. It's my first home, my mother, and I'll cherish and care for it, but I still want to leave it."

He was astonished, and so was I. "If it's possible in my lifetime, I intend to go and live beyond planet earth. What's more, I'd like to keep going; I don't mean just to circle the earth in a capsule, I'd like to go beyond the solar system. I want to meet other life. If scientists or psychics learn how to teach us to extend our lives, I'll extend mine. If it becomes possible to change the corruptible flesh to incorruptible, as St. Paul said, I'll do it. If it's possible, I'll not sleep; I'll be changed, and 'death shall have no dominion.' " Jonas was horrified.

As we were parting that evening, I said, half seriously, "Jonas, you can have earth."

"Well, what does that leave you?"

"The universe!"

We were both stunned by the conversation. Later I told him it was like a Greek drama between earth people and cosmic people. Possibly we were witnessing the natural diversification of the species at this phase, to meet the requirement for some to be attracted to new and vital tasks of nurturing, tending, and bringing harmony to earth—what Teilhard calls "the agents of planetisation"—the "builders of the earth," and for some to be attracted to going beyond earth to build new worlds, and be transformed into new beings—extraterrestrials and new terrestrials—builders of "new heavens and a new earth": new worlds on earth, new worlds in space. I think they'll be complementary and mutually supportive.

I learned from Jonas' rejection of universal life, and Abe Maslow's disinterest in the physical aspect of universal development that a philosophy was needed that included their aspirations, even though theirs didn't include mine and those like mine. Through the challenge of those men, whom I so deeply admired, whose work is seminal in their fields, I found myself trying to develop a philosophy of synthesis and inclusion and empathy for those of different inclinations and temperaments. I tried to gain an emotional stand toward the various functions, roles, and characters of people, which didn't require them to accept my vision of transformation in order for me to accept portions of the vision they saw. That is, I tried to identify emotionally with the experience of wholeness.

I began to feel I was broader than anyone I knew. It was hard for me to accept. I was so accustomed to looking upon experts as superior. Each "great man" I knew—Jonas, Abe Maslow, Earl, Lance Whyte, Thomas Merton—closed some doors in his mind that were open to me. I saw connections everywhere. I related the parts of humankind to the whole of humankind, and humankind to the whole evolving universe. I saw everything in terms of phases, of processes leading to major evolutionary changes. The integration of society on earth, the care of basic needs of all people, the emancipation of individual potential, the expansion of consciousness, the physical life extension, and the extraterrestrial development were all the natural characteristics of a planetary species at the historical point of transformation from earth-only toward its universal phase of development.

Perhaps I was experiencing "feminine consciousness," which sees things whole intuitively. God knows, my intellect was racing to catch up with my intuition, always lagging behind the "signals." The hunger of Eve had led me toward a wholistic vision. It dawned on me that there might be some comprehensive enabling role to play.

This attitude was strengthened by the developments in "The Center Letter." The responses reinforced the recognition that people were seeing fragments, and I was publishing fragments, even reinforcing fragmentation. I didn't have the strength to communicate a wholistic view in that letter. I had so far failed to create a context in which people could discover how the parts fit into the evolving whole. I found that the essence of the experience of *being* part of the body of humankind was not communicable by the written word alone.

I couldn't even tell people personally when they loved me, if it conflicted with their viewpoint or temperamental difference. I came to another impasse. Even if it's true that the planet is integrating into one body and being born toward universal life, I had failed to communicate it by putting it down as clearly as I could in a book. I had failed to communicate it by creating a letter and subtly trying to get people by osmosis to believe or experience the oneness and the birth. I had failed to persuade the best minds I knew, Jonas Salk and Abraham Maslow, that this was organically natural.

I've been completely transformed by an inner motivation.

During "The Center Letter" era, I discovered some "brother and sister evolutionaries" who hadn't yet made their mark in the world. One was George T. Lock Land, who has subsequently written a great work called *Grow or Die, the Unifying Principle of Transformation.* George's model deepened my understanding of the birth model. The "naturalness" of this phase of coming together from independence toward interdependence was a phenomenon observed in all nature. It helped me understand why fusing of differences works better today than the replicative acts wherein you try to impose yourself on someone else to make that person like you. Also, George's model reinforces the conviction that it's now necessary to begin establishing a new beachhead in outer space, for this planet is integrating and beginning to consume its own sources of energy very rapidly.

I came across the writings of Sri Aurobindo, who is to Eastern religion what Teilhard de Chardin is to Western Christianity. We were living through a "crisis of transformation" and could become "conscious collaborators of our own evolution." Aurobindo and an extraordinary French woman of psychic powers, who came to be known as the Mother, created an ashram in Pondicherry, India, and began a new "planetary city" called Auroville, whose purpose is to facilitate the evolution of mankind.

When I discovered their work, I immediately wrote to the Mother in Pondicherry and published quotes from their magazine *Equals One.* I sent her a copy of the manuscript *The Birth of Mankind.* She sent back a cruel letter, written by her secretary,

since she was very old at that time, saying it was ludicrous to
suggest, as Earl does in the book, that "the search is on." She said
anyone who has a deep experience of truth already knows the
intention of creation. We're *not* searching. We *know*. I wrote back:
"Even if you're right, any person with a deep knowledge of the
creative intention, or God, wouldn't slap down a seeker who was
trying."

Aurobindo and the Mother believed it's possible to transform
bodies at the cellular level by direct psychic communication, creating new bodies impervious to death. However, they scorned man-
made physical extensions—telephone, television, rockets, modern
media—as "unnatural," causing the atrophy of our "natural capabilities." They skipped one step—the transitional need for scientific-
technological tools of transcendence, the first-stage methods. They
tried to evolve directly from Homo sapiens to Homo universalis by
psychic powers alone. It didn't work. They both died, although the
Mother tried not to by conscious psychic transformation of her
own cells toward an incorruptible state.

I read Aurobindo on the beach of Nantucket on vacation with
Earl and the children. Although I wanted to be with the children—
loving, carefree, playful—this driving hunger blocked me; I felt cut
off from empathy with the whole body. I was really trying for
direct contact with the "supramental." So I read about the early life
of Aurobindo. Evidentally, he didn't prepare his political speeches.
He "knew" what to do and what to say, entering deep-level trances
and at the same time powerful action. I took long walks on the
beach, trying to make, or let, that happen to me, following yoga
techniques as best I could understand them from the book, focusing on a single thought, clearing my mind, meditating. Nothing
happened. I couldn't get a direct signal. It was very distressing.

I brooded deeply about why I couldn't continue to receive direct signals. I'd had the great birth experience, but all the other
signals were so unclear. It occurred to me there might be a reason
other than my own lack of spiritual development. We're entering
an age of democratization of awareness. Perhaps the mode will be

one of gradual knowing, rather than sudden psychic experience. We'll enter a new norm that becomes continual. I can look back over my own growth as one of a very slow dawning of the light, rather than one of the kind of events that continually happened to the great mystics. I've been denied their kind of continuity of mystical experience—which I longed for in the hope of being *absolutely* certain I was under the commandment of God and not my own whims.

Yet, when I look back on my whole life, I've been completely transformed by an inner motivation from the pattern of life that guided that girl in Scarsdale. I had learned no reliable skills of meditation or yoga. I was figuring out the way to evolutionary "collaboration" through vocation, or work, which isn't sufficient. I've consistently resisted immersing myself in efforts of consciousness expansion. Jean Houston, one of the most brilliant and powerful women I know, the director of the Foundation for Mind Research, once said to me: "Barbara, you're barely tapping your own creativity. You're living off the surface of your mind." She practically commanded me to work with her to break through the barriers to creativity. I resisted (perhaps wrongly) because my temptation is so great to enter an altered state of consciousness— and stay there—that I fear if I did achieve "enlightenment" through direct means, I would, as Plato put it, "be unwilling to descend to human affairs: for their souls [enlightened people] are ever hastening into the upper world where they desire to dwell" (*The Republic*).

Late in 1968 I decided to stop publishing "The Center Letter," although I was enjoying the personal satisfaction of meeting people —I had a "salon." Correspondents were in touch worldwide. When they came to New York we would meet; I had a series of auto-intoxicating encounters. We affirmed each other, but the results of our meetings were evanescent, and finally appeared to me as self-indulgent.

I prepared my last letter in December 1968: "The Cathedral of Action." I felt we were really building a cathedral of action but couldn't *see* it, because there wasn't any structure to fit our separate acts together. I envisioned a structure with three pillars of action converging at the peak like the spire of a cathedral—or a rocket: freedom, union, and transcendence. The basic idea was that each of us is part of a process of transformation, which will organically produce greater freedom, union, and transcendence for all. I desperately wanted people to *see* the beauty of their acts put together as a whole.

This letter was by far the most effective in the series of eight. It was more appealing than *The Birth of Mankind* for most people, because I didn't force anyone to accept anything, yet I created a context in which they were all there as acts. They weren't required to like each other or agree with each other. People sent for copies from all over the world. Mrs. Aldous Huxley bought a hundred for Christmas cards. It was a celebration of the beauty of each act as part of the whole. But, still, nothing happened—or so it appeared to me.

If more *people were* for *people*. . . .

That Christmas season, 1968, Apollo 8 circled the moon. Frank Borman read from Genesis: "In the beginning God created the heaven and the earth. . . ." For the first time the world saw itself as one body with the same eye at the same time from the same place. It was a momentous moment for humankind, and it was experienced throughout the entire body of earth—bringing us closer to a corporate birth experience than through any other event. It caused some people to experience what I had—our oneness and birth into the universe.

That same Christmas Eve, Earl, the children, Mademoiselle Baldet, and I were flying to New Mexico for a meeting of Up with

People, a group of young women and men, assembled from many nations, who were composing and performing a new music of hope.

A year before, our eldest daughter Suzanne had decided to join Up with People. They came to sing at Hotchkiss in Lakeville. Suzanne was then at Fox Hollow Boarding School in Lenox, Massachusetts. A neighbor had called me, asking if I'd put up two or three of the young people at my house. I said I'd be glad to. She wasn't sure who they were, except they were travelling the world, singing about the future and the potential of people. I was immediately interested.

I found in the young women an element I hadn't seen before in any group. They were totally positive, full of confidence that people could create a new future. They wrote their own music to celebrate possibilities. They didn't seem to be following a particular dogma or religion. (Several years before, the group had separated from Moral Rearmament, a Christian-based movement attempting to save the world through following the ethical commandments of Christ.)

I was excited by their hopefulness, so I called Suzanne and asked her to try to get excused for the concert. "I have a feeling it's something you should hear." She managed to get away, and we picked her up and went directly to the auditorium at Hotchkiss. Suzanne was then sixteen, restless and rebellious at Foxhollow. Yet the alternative schools experimenting in various life-styles, such as Putney, were turning out serious cases of psychological breakdown, people who couldn't tolerate the frustration of the world at all. As far as I knew there was no school that taught a student to become a part of conscious evolution, a builder of the future. I had an intuition that Up with People might offer real opportunity for her.

The Up with People cast came charging down the aisles; they ran onto the stage and began to sing their theme song:

> Up, up with people,
> you meet them wherever you go;
> up, up with people;

they are the best kind of folks you know;
if *more* people were *for* people,
for people everywhere;
there'd be lots less people to worry about
and lots more people who care. . . .

(© Up with People)

The magic was the genuine motivation and the irresistible beat of enthusiasm. Suzanne was excited by the spirit. After the performance, we talked to members of the cast who circulated among the faculty and young men of Hotchkiss. Suzanne asked, "How do you join?" The adults who were organizing the event said, "We need you. Just come with us." That was amazing. No red tape, no credentials, no qualifications—only motivation. Yet the young people of all colors and backgrounds looked healthy, vigorous, clean, exuberant. They were travelling all over the country in buses; it was obviously a major organizational effort. Suzanne immediately asked Earl and me if she could join them, and we agreed to let her go.

She joined a "sing-out" and invited us shortly after to join her and Cast A in Milwaukee. Earl, Wade, Alex, Stephanie, Lloyd, Mademoiselle, and I attended a large performance of several thousand people in the Milwaukee Stadium that night; it was brightly lit as if for a baseball game. The cast of young people were the players, pushing their energy to the limit to reach the hearts of their audience with the basic message that "within every person there is someone bigger who wants to be born."

Suzanne's description of the interpersonal relations among the cast made ordinary classroom relationships seem barbaric. "At school we were always working to get credits," she said, making a face, "or to get better marks than someone else, but here, we forget about *self* and think about reaching out to others. Everyone helps everyone else. And we advise each other without worrying about hurting each others' feelings."

She took us to a "Green Room" meeting of the cast. Various young people got up to encourage the whole group. Then one of the "superstars," as Suzanne calls the great singers, said, "Let's have a minute of silence and try to harness our thoughts into one." We bowed our heads, and I felt the power of united aspirations linking me to these strangers and to my own daughter in a way I had never experienced before.

Suzanne introduced us at one of the cast meetings. Standing up, unasked, she said, "I want to introduce you to my parents, who are the most wonderful mother and father anyone could have." Then Earl made a speech on the artist as a maker of images of transcendence. He said Up with People was representing an "evangelism of the future."

That night Suzanne talked to us for hours. She said her desire to star, to lead, had been given a good outlet. "I had to decide whether I was going to be the 'naughtiest kid on the block,' or do my best. It was a life-or-death decision. The minute I saw the cast come on the stage at Hotchkiss, I knew that was my chance for life. I decided to do everything I could to get it."

She told them about our work; I mailed a copy of *The Birth of Mankind* to Blanton Belk, the head of the organization. They were immediately responsive to the philosophy of birth and hope, and invited Earl and his family to join them in New Mexico, where Suzanne and hundreds of others were congregating for the Christmas season. They invited Earl to speak there.

It was a significant cluster of events to me—Apollo 8 was circling the moon and for the first time we were invited for the sake of our own work to meet with a group of people dedicating their total energy to awakening in others hopeful action for the future. Also, "The Cathedral of Action" was out in the world, my first effort to synthesize the action for change into a new whole.

Earl gave his speech the first evening we were there. As he arose, they began to sing directly to him, for him, celebrating his work on behalf of mankind. Earl, who had been working alone for so many years, was deeply moved and gave an extemporaneous talk plus questions and answers, which finally became the introduction to *The Birth of Mankind*. When he finished they sang to him again.

The next day Buckminster Fuller spoke. He walked to the stage, a small man in a halo of light. Before he could speak, they began to sing one of their great hits: "What color is God's skin? It's black, yellow, red, it's brown and it's white; everyone's the same in the good Lord's sight." Every time I think of this I cry. He stood there, tears running down his cheeks; he simply couldn't talk. Finally, in a voice barely audible, he said, "I want you to know, there *is* a God."

I had never heard him use that word before—this great evolutionary engineer and poet. He was affirming the faith of the young people who were affirming his work. Fuller is notifying humanity that our destiny is to become a total success by working with the laws of the universe. We, humanity, can understand evolutionary processes and co-create a world system in which every person will be free to emancipate their creative potential, to become universal citizens, stewards of evolution, both on this planet and in the "local universe."

Up with People offered total affirmation of the reality of this hope. Coming from the young in sound, it reached directly to the heart. Words and philosophy communicate with the mind and are essential, but they don't touch the emotions, particularly abstract philosophy such as Buckminster Fuller, Teilhard de Chardin, and Abraham Maslow wrote. This total affirmation in music was overwhelming to those in whom the flame of expectation burns. I'm not the only person who responded to Up with People this way. Audiences as a whole wept. I've seen adults in Italy, France, Germany, completely transformed by this joy, which is spiritual and evolutionary with an allusion to the God force at the core.

Up with People invited us to travel abroad with them to Italy. The following spring we accompanied them to Europe. We went in a large jet financed by some corporation, with all their guitars, musical instruments, costumes, lights. Up with People groups were forming throughout Europe. The Americans learned the language of the countries, to sing in Italy, Spain, France; then the young people of the country would form their own Up with People song groups. I remember one tiny town in Italy, not far from Milan. There was to be an Up with People performance by Italian youngsters in a small hillside village outside Milan. We drove with an older couple to a village schoolhouse in the hills. We walked in and the music began; it was in Italian—the same experience there. The power of that affirmation was tremendous. I wanted to be able to give everything I had to broaden that simple message in song to include philosophy, science, and politics.

They indicated they were going to use Earl as their spokesman to the press and elsewhere. However, they didn't. This was another instance of something *almost* clicking. Earl spoke with each group (three casts were touring Europe). He told them that in Europe a spark of freedom had been ignited that had now travelled around the earth and was moving forward toward the universe. He spoke magnificently. But whatever the reason—perhaps the philosophy was more specific than they were ready to espouse—we weren't given the opportunity to speak to the press for them as promised. I can understand that in retrospect. They were winning support from everyone through stimulation of feeling, and they were successful; why should they risk it with a philosophy that was controversial?

There was a scene I'll never forget at the large square in Italy. Two main buildings stood on either side of an immense piazza. On one side was the Catholic church, and on the other was the Communist mayor's residence. The red flag of the Communist party flew in front of the mayor's office on one side of this ocean of space; on the other continent was the cathedral. The young people were singing on the steps in front of the mayor's building with the red flag flying above them. The square filled with multitudes of people. When they began, "What color is God's skin?" the bishop in his red robe stepped out of the cathedral, and the mayor appeared at the same moment. Both joined in singing "What color is God's skin?" in Italian. A Communist mayor, a Catholic bishop, all the Italians, and all the young Americans—I have to stop crying— the agnostics, the atheists, the different religions; it didn't make the slightest difference, because the truth was greater than any of those

divisions. You could see it there in that picture of the Catholics and
the Communists and the young and the old and the black and the
white; it made no difference. They were one—we were one. We
had a common future. When that music played, I don't think anyone could have resisted it. The feeling created a magnetic field of
unity that I've come to experience time after time in certain situations. This was the first time I recognized others feeling the same
sense of being part of the evolutionary process and of mankind.

Then something happened to Up with People: They became
"popular," their songs were excellent, their performance outstanding, stars were born among them. They took anyone who wanted
to go. They weren't looking for talent, they were looking for motivation, but some of the most beautiful young singers I've ever
heard surfaced. They were on television with Bob Hope, sponsored
by Coca-Cola and Pan-Am; they were recognized. The astronauts
came to see them. The raw talent that came off the streets and the
schools was being transformed into a highly professional singing
team. They developed a rock beat instead of the straightforward
gospel beat of rising hope. When I saw them subsequently I felt
that some of the power was gone. They had become too perfect,
too professional. It was as though the meaning was bleached out of
them prematurely.

However, it was a tremendous experience. I know as time goes
on, there'll be meetings and places and times to celebrate this oneness and transcendence. The new rituals of this age are being created by such groups as Up with People.

I felt united to my own past.

After our exciting meeting with Up with People, I sent *The
Birth of Mankind* to Stewart Lancaster, editor of *Pace* magazine.
We received a letter within the week: "This is a magnificent book

—we would be proud to publish it." They changed the name to *The Search Is On.* (*Pace* was published by Up with People.)

Earlier, when I was starting "The Center Letter" in late 1967, I had met Ed Cornish, who founded the World Future Society and publishes *The Futurist*. Ed and I moved into the public area at the same time. He was working for the National Geographic Society as a science writer. He started *The Futurist*, circulating a mimeographed sheet mainly to people in business management, general systems, urban planning, technology assessment, forecasting, the future in general. It was a different kind of group than "The Center Letter" correspondents—technologically oriented, "pragmatists," and preponderantly male.

He invited me to be on the board of the World Future Society, along with Carl Madden, chief economist of the U.S. Chamber of Commerce; Dr. Glenn Seaborg and Michael Michaelis of Arthur D. Little; Arnold Barach, editor of *Changing Times*; Orville Freeman, who had been secretary of agriculture under Kennedy. I'm the only woman, and also the only nonprofessional person on the board. I asked Ed why he chose me. "You have a different kind of wisdom, which I think we need," he replied.

Ed is one of the few people I know who took a leap without being sanctioned by any other authority. Shortly after he started *The Futurist*, he was offered a more responsible job with the National Geographic Society. He had to make a choice—if he took the more responsible position, he'd have less time to work on building the World Future Society and publishing *The Futurist*. With no independent income, and no guarantees, he left the National Geographic and gave his full time to building the World Future Society; his wife, Sally, worked devotedly with him. Ed is modest, mild, unassuming, and has a single purpose: to provide a forum for ideas on the future. He doesn't take a stand on ideas.

We are complementary but different. My desire was, and is, to advocate a future based on global society and universal life. His desire is to provide an open forum for all concepts. Both are necessary. *The Futurist* is now the outstanding publication in the field.

Both he and *Pace* published excerpts from *The Birth of Man-*

kind before it became a book. Excerpts were also published in
Clarence Streit's magazine *Freedom and Union,* the publication of
his organization Federal Union, which promotes a federal union of
the democracies as the next political step toward freedom and
order on a global scale.

A compulsive worker, unable not to work, I decided to do for
myself what I had done for Earl. I went through my journals and
typed by hand 800 pages of excerpts, only one-fourth of the total
verbiage—good God! As I went through my own life, typing what
I considered to be the nuggets—800 pages of nuggets—I relived
it.

I wrote in my journal, "I'm grateful to the girl that I was, that
she never gave up." If she had given up, I wouldn't exist. I was
different from that girl who had gone to Bryn Mawr and had lived
in Lime Rock and Lakeville. She had been trapped in an old concept of reality. I was free to evolve a new concept of life. My
gratitude to her endurance was boundless. I felt united to my own
past. I was detached from it but loved it and myself, in a strange
way—as though I were loving someone else.

After typing the 800 pages, even I knew it was too much. I had
met a soulmate, Eleanor Garst, who had helped me do some of the
reading and editing for "The Center Letter." I asked her to read
through the 800 pages and help me edit the excerpts into a book.
Eleanor took a suitcase full of the typed material and together we
edited *The Chosen Life, an Experiment in Freedom.*

I started the usual efforts to get published and met with the
usual rejection. Finally I found a publisher that expressed interest
in it—a West Coast publisher of mystical works. I hesitated, not
wanting to be identified with occultism of any kind. Just then we
received word that Earl's book was to be published, so I decided to
hold back on mine, since having it published by a mystical press at
that time might be harmful.

Earl and I had become accustomed to in-depth dialogue in the
development of the first book. While I was editing "The Center
Letter," doing my own book, and meeting all these people, I was
continuing my dialogues with Earl. A new book began to emerge

in my mind for him: *The Need for New Worlds.* I finished that one later—it was never published; I never tried. Subsequently Earl revised and elaborated it. Then it was published in 1975 as *The Creative Intention.*

However, events overtook both my efforts to publish *The Chosen Life* and *The Need for New Worlds.* It was 1969, and I had stopped publishing "The Center Letter." NASA was preparing for the lunar landing. I had become evermore interested in the space program as an expression of the physical aspect of universal life.

When the landing on. the moon occurred, I, like millions of others, stayed up all night. My experience in watching the rocket take off on television was hysterical joy, completely beyond the ordinary. I *identified* with the rocket! I felt myself rising in space, breaking through the cocoon of the sky and moving into the universe. I had felt the same joy at the birth of my own babies. I cried uncontrollably as it rose into space, the words "freedom, freedom, freedom" pounding in my head. I was so embarrassed I had to leave the room. It was about 4:00 A.M. in Lakeville; the capsule had landed on the moon; the door of the lunar module opened and Neil Armstrong backed down the ladder, toward that famous first human step upon a new world.

Even the mass media responded. Walter Cronkite was thrilled. It seemed to break through the infantile nervous system for a second, although they reported it as an exciting, costly spectacular. Man-in-the-street interviews were given around the world. The major excitement was expressed by the "common" citizen. The intellectual was holding back, saying, "Well, this money could have better been spent on earth; here we are with the Civil Rights movement, people starving, and the United States spent this money to show off, or how dare we put an American flag on the moon, or this was just an act to beat the Russians."

That very day, July 20, 1969, *The Search Is On* was published. When you think of its long and arduous history, that's a remarkable coincidence. The birth experience was affirmed in real time on the very day the book was born into the world.

5

I was overjoyed at the lunar landing. At last, the story could be told. Everyone already knew! We had all experienced our oneness and birth. We had come through the danger. The placenta had been pierced. The waters had broken. The rocket had risen, spewing fire and water—a tiny sliver lifting from the giant, magnetic hold of earth. The cosmic child had touched the breast of the moon, that wonderful ancient rock, so full of minerals and resources, that would soon provide a new source of nourishment as we stopped depleting our mother earth.

But, after the first few instants of feeling the joy of oneness, the pain of oneness intensified. Mankind screamed. "Bad news" flashed through the nervous system. Everything hurt. The birth was a mistake. NASA spent too much. We should be minding our business on earth. The sense of defeat and despair deepened. The Civil Rights movement was increasing in intensity; "flower children" were taking drugs; students were rioting, locking up deans and

Totality

sensing loss of relevance. Political leadership was floundering instead of announcing a new age of cooperation that required the involvement of all people. Some prophets asserted that knowledge, science, technology, the rationalism of the West, and civilization itself were wrong. We should withdraw and return to some past (womb) state. Perhaps the whole enterprise of humanity was a failure. The voices of hope were silent.

When I became totally committed,
I became totally free.

Everything I had done was pitifully ineffective. I felt a failure. I *had* to think of something different, something new, to do. I worried that mankind might destroy itself for lack of awareness and hope.

Once again that blessed driving anger fueled me with the strength for action. As at the death of my mother, as at my own psychological death in Lime Rock, as at the slaughter of hope in the arts at the Museum of Modern Art, now again the rage for life took over. I sensed mankind like a newborn child being whipped before my eyes by those who said we couldn't make it. My response was instinctive: I rushed in to help.

Since I had already experienced the personal connection between my "self" and mankind, I didn't even feel I was "helping" someone else. Self-preservation not self-sacrifice was the motivation—really a new pragmatism. If humankind self-destructs, all its members suffer: To care for yourself pragmatically you must care for the whole.

That anger, born of love for life, caused something to "click" to the broader channel. More information is received on the channel of empathy, as had happened, for example, during the birth experience on the hill. Feeling this empathy, I had already made a total commitment to help humankind get through this dangerous ten to twenty years of critical "infancy" as a planetary system trying to coordinate itself. It wasn't even a willed decision. Like the original hunger, like falling in—and out—of love, like the epiphany, it was a given fact.

I took a walk on the Lakeville hill and spoke out loud to myself, as I often did—a clear dialogue between a guiding voice and a responsive servant: "You'll commit yourself totally for the life of mankind. It's not enough to 'tell the story' of our birth in words or at luncheon parties. You have to go out into the world and find out how to communicate with mankind. You've got to *do* something. You have to put everything else second—children, Earl, money, your own comfort. Go!"

"All right, I will. I want to. I know it's right."

I told my children, whom I love dearly, that their mother was a pioneer; I had to go forth and find a way to create a new way of being; they could come, too, as soon as I'd created an open place, if they wanted to. This place would be open to anyone who chose to come. Their response was heartening. Wade, then nine, said something I'll never forget. One night, as I was tucking him in, I told him, "I'm afraid I may appear to be a poor mother for some time, but I want you to know I love you."

Wade quickly put my fears to rest. "Mummy, you're doing what a mother's suppose to do—you're making the future. That's what mothers are supposed to do. And we know you love us."

Earl, however, tried to persuade me I was mistaken to try to become an organizer. "Barbara, we must be *used* by organizers to give them ideas."

"But, Earl—no one is asking us! We could sit around and wait the rest of our lives to be asked. No! We've got to take the initiative. You're wrong to want the world to come to you. We've got to reach out to others."

In some way I had earned the right to this total commitment. I had been constant in my dedication to Earl and the development of his ideas, and I had established my love for the children. I think they interpreted my commitment as a sign of love for them as well as for me and mankind.

Suzanne was already in the world. By this time Stephanie had also decided to join Up with People. Wade, Alexandra, and Lloyd had Mademoiselle Baldet as well as me, so they were never at any time afraid of being left alone or rejected. I thank God for her presence. I wouldn't have been able to go forth if I had had to leave them uncared for. I probably would have taken them with me. Of course, there were occasional volcanic eruptions of resentment; my attention was magnetized elsewhere. I resented it, too. Sometimes I asked for release, for rest, not to feel the pull—but it never went away. I couldn't concentrate for long on anything but this strange mission. Mademoiselle was a critical, loving link with the children during those few years while Suzanne and Stephanie were teenagers and Lloyd, Wade, and Alex were children.

I didn't know what I was going to do, but I knew I'd changed, that I'd never be the same person again; I'd never be bound by any pattern that prevented me from doing my best to bring options of hope into the communications system. There was a total hunger to do it, and I had nothing else to do. It's a wonderful, coherent state of being. There's a paradox about it: When I became totally committed, I became totally free—a depth of freedom I'd never known. I was free of self-doubt, self-constraint, confusion, pride, fear. The worldly world had no hold on me. This freedom comes from opening yourself totally to the full force of the unique life urge within you, the part of your being that "knows" who you are and is connected somehow with the larger flow of generic, planetary changes. Creative force become operative in you on a larger scale. It's like riding a bicycle: All the parts of your body know what to do without telling them. You're free to ride where you please.

The hardest part was the thought that I might neglect my children. It's easier to separate psychologically from a man you've loved than from the children you've borne. I couldn't, and didn't, and never will separate myself psychologically from them, even though, for a brief time, I had to be away. But what I did was develop an additional role. While I was still their biological mother, I took on a larger motherhood—I don't like to say for the whole of mankind, because that sounds presumptuous, but, given the experience of each one of us being a member of the whole body, it truly was impossible for me to say I was working for anything but the whole of mankind.

There was something ludicrous about a woman with no professional skills, no reputation, a series of continual rejections, deciding to undertake something for mankind, such as to communicate to it that it is one body being born into the universe. The immensity of the task, its unusual nature, and my inadequacy struck me as ridiculous. But it didn't matter. That's another part of the freedom of total commitment. You don't have to give up your reputation with the powers that be; you don't have to prove to the intellectuals that you're smart. You're freed from all that. You're under a new order, a new dispensation.

I racked my brain about what to do. NASA, the great agency of transcendence—what Earl called "our stairway to the stars"—was being maligned. The genius of engineers, scientists, astronauts, systems, was being scattered. The skilled builders of new worlds were fired, unemployed, driving taxis. The people didn't understand what they were losing—their arms, their legs, their eyes, for the universe—their life. Their future was being taken away.

I couldn't stand it. There was one woman I knew who might help—Lady Malcolm Douglas-Hamilton, an American widow of a Scotsman, who lived in New York. She had organized Bundles for Britain during the war and was now setting up The Center of American Living, with which I helped her. Her main theme was to affirm cultural excellence in the United States.

I took her to lunch at the Westbury Hotel on Madison Avenue. "Natalie," I said, drawing a deep breath. (I knew that space and global oneness were *not* her interest.) "I've made up my mind that the future of human culture and excellence depends on the continuation of the space program!" An odd idea for 1969. "We've got to *do* something!"

She responded immediately. "Barbara, why don't we have a space meeting? Let's get the civic leaders of the country together with the space leaders and try for a new national commitment to keep going forward."

"Great, Natalie, let's do it! We'll put Earl up there with the space leaders to talk about the need for new worlds, since they'll never do it on their own."

I hugged her, and we ordered a bottle of wine to toast "Victory in Space" (her title). Then we hurried to her apartment, got out the card files, and began to make lists of heads of organizations: the General Federation of Women's Clubs, the Church Women United, the Boy Scouts, the Girl Scouts, etc. I listed Werhner von Braun, Neil Armstrong, Frank Borman, John Glenn—I'd never met any of them or even seen a rocket in the flesh. She wrote to the civic leaders and I wrote to the space leaders. I went home then and triumphantly told Earl what I'd done.

"It'll never work," he said. "Those people won't accept me."

"Earl, stop thinking in such narrow terms. We're trying to *make something happen,* not get you accepted."

I remembered the exciting days of the discovery of the "evolutionary idea" as I wrote to everyone in the aerospace field, inviting him to participate. One of the letters fell on the desk of Colonel John Whiteside, who was chief officer of information for the air force in New York City. John was asked to look into the conference to see "if there is something for the air force in it." He turned the assignment over to a young captain in his office, William Knowlton, asking him to find out about Barbara Hubbard and the meeting. Bill, it turned out, was a neighbor of ours in Lakeville, Connecticut, and that weekend he came to visit us. We held forth on the meaning of space and the future of mankind. He was excited by the ideas, and said, "You've got to meet my colonel. He's a spellbinder, and maybe he'll help." He went back and told John that we should meet.

On September 25, 1969, Lt. Colonel John Whiteside came to lunch at the New York apartment. My meeting with him was similar to my first meeting with Jonas. He opened the door; we looked directly into each other's eyes, and there it was—instant recognition. He was wearing an air force uniform and had an extraterrestrial look in his eyes—but he was looking very personally at me; he was also very "worldly."

John was medium height and solidly built, with the strong body of a man who had worked on a farm and in a coal mine during the depression to help his family. He came from West Frankfort, Illinois, from a Southern Baptist family. At forty-eight his face was weathered, lined—masculine and sexy: there are no other words for it. He was a man who knew women easily. A look of self-confidence, intelligence, exuberance, and natural leadership charmed me. He had the top non-Pentagon position as chief officer of information in New York, where he worked with the mass media —NBC, CBS, ABC. His life was in the mainstream of national affairs.

During lunch Earl spent most of the time talking. I probably had the tape recorder on, because I was always the one taping conversations. After lunch we sat on the sofa while Earl was still eloquently describing the meaning of the space program.

"You know what it's really like, John?" I said. "It's like birth. We're going to be universal."

Those grey-green extraterrestrial eyes caressed my whole body. "That's right, we are." He smiled; there it was! The magnets had turned their currents on again; we were together. "It's amazing," he said. "I spent years down at the Cape—I've seen hundreds of launches; I got the live coverage accepted. I know—most of us knew—that what we were doing meant something. But no one could say *what*. It's like reporting the birth of Christ in terms of the labor problems at the inn, the cost of food, and how much the baby weighed. But how did you come to this?" He looked at me. "You don't know one end of a rocket from the other."

"Purpose," I said. "I discovered it through my search for meaning. But now I know it's not enough to talk about it. People like us outside the space program—citizens—have to begin to act. They've got advocates for every disease, every need, but not for the future of humanity. We've got to learn how to communicate *meaning* for the future."

He nodded. "That's very interesting. During the sixties we knew how to communicate ideas in the air force, but ever since Woodstock, something has changed. People have different antennae up—it's more selective. They're tuning out what they don't want to hear and listening for something new. You don't even need a high energy signal. If it's the right message, it'll get through; if they don't want to hear it, they won't." He laughed. "You know what I'm trying to communicate now? The C-5, the F-111, and the Vietnam War. I have to sneak my generals out back doors. There's no credibility."

I could see he had come to the end of his rope.

Bill Knowlton called after the meeting and said that Colonel Whiteside wanted twelve copies of *The Search Is On*. I called John then, and asked him to help us with the space meeting.

He agreed instantly. "Let's do it, Barbara!"

I knew I'd found the person I needed—an activist who knew the ways of the world. We began to work together. He took over the organization of the meeting, the invitations, the media contacts.

My life transformed again. The meeting with John occurred three months after I'd made the total commitment. (This is an insight for all evolutionaries: Always dare to initiate; when you do, what you need will be provided, as long as what you're doing is for the good of the whole.)

In my amazement at having found a person with the characteristics needed to bring these ideas into the mainstream, I began to have in-depth conversations with John. We had a long talk one November afternoon in the St. Regis Hotel.

"John, you can do this; it's in you," I said.

He knew that was true, but he said, "I don't feel I have the character, the high standards of morality, the background, to undertake a task like this."

I disagreed completely. "I think your so-called worldly weaknesses may prove to be a strength. No one is going to think you're self-righteous and perfect." He had all the typical attributes of his way of life—drinking, partying, women. But, somehow, I knew that would be a help. Also, I had been surrounded by self-righteous men and had come *not* to admire that kind of perfection.

John struggled both to accept this totality and not to. But in some strange way his life had been a preparation for it. He had accumulated a remarkable set of talents. He had wanted to be a minister, but couldn't get a "sign from the Lord." He went to Southern Illinois University for two years and married a college friend, Francis. In World War II he entered the air force, like everyone believing deeply in the defense of freedom and in the morality of his acts. Then a short career setting up his own successful advertising firm followed. A search for commitment—Communism—Alice Bailey-type occultism? No. Called back during the Korean War he reached the top of his profession in the sixties as public information officer. He told the media the truth, and they trusted him. He went beyond his authority to press for live coverage of the Apollo shots, and succeeded—then the meaning ran out of his life. The space program was misunderstood. The military had lost its purpose of defense. It was the age of overkill; the "game" became obviously insane.

John was driving himself to slow destruction, squandering his energy, because, like me, he couldn't live without meaning. (How many can?) We began to be ever more closely attracted, working together continually on the space meeting. Obviously our effort would have to extend beyond a single event. The more we did together, the harder it became for him not to be as total as I. The combination of the need for meaning, our growing love, and the sense of global timing fused toward a decision.

On Christmas Eve, 1969, I was standing by the fire in Lakeville, surrounded by Earl and the children, sorting out the Christmas stockings, looking at the Christmas tree we'd decorated on December 22, my fortieth birthday. The phone rang—it was John.

"Barbara, I've decided to do it. I'm going to give my life to this."

A great weight lifted from my shoulders; I could feel the sense of lightening. My shoulders straightened, and I breathed deeply and stretched my body to full height. My eighteen-year-old fear of being forty and having nothing to do but bake bread flashed through my mind. "Thank you, John. I knew you would." I could say no more with everyone there. Gratitude flooded me, and, as at all moments of great happiness for me, I started to cry.

The children clustered at my side. "What's the matter, Mummy?"

"It's nothing, children, except I'm so happy, and I love you all so much." I put my arms around them in an awkward embrace and wouldn't let go until they practically shouted to Earl for help.

We went to the space meeting on February 18, 1970, at the Roosevelt Hotel in New York City. On the platform was Frank Borman, the astronaut who had circled the moon; Krafft Ehricke, philosopher and long-range space planner of North American Rockwell; Dr. Harold Ritchey, president of Thiokol Chemical Corporation and developer of the solid fuel propellants for the rockets; Chester Lee, who was later Apollo mission director and

Skylab director; Hugh Downs, the TV star; Bob Considine, the columnist; and Earl Hubbard. In the audience were heads of national organizations—about 200 people.

But the meeting was a disaster. Civic leaders didn't understand the language of the space leaders; the space leaders spoke in quantitative terms in the language of their discipline; they didn't know how to relate their great act directly to the needs or imagination of the other people in that audience. Earl, who had been placed on this platform by Natalie, John, and me, was unknown to any of the space or civic leaders, and came from a totally different background and root of thought. His language was so utterly different from theirs that his speech, "The Need for New Worlds," hung there like an unattached jewel in space—it didn't appear to relate directly to anyone. None of the space leaders were saying we needed new worlds; certainly no civic leaders were concerned with the need for building new communities and habitats in space, much less "universal life."

When the speeches were over, Hugh Downs asked for questions: there was none; people were too stunned or bored or both. Hugh asked and answered a few questions himself to overcome the embarrassing pause. I was a nervous wreck, thinking once again with a sinking heart that this wasn't the way. There was no communication between the languages of philosophy, science, and civic affairs.

Directly after the meeting, Jim Sparks, who had been working with us to put together the meeting, said, "Barbara, invite Dr. Ritchey to dinner."

I had never even talked to Dr. Ritchey. He's a distinguished scientist, head of a large corporation, an abstract speaker. Not knowing what else to do, and having no reason not to, I went over to him: "Would you come to dinner?"

He immediately said yes. "Not only that," he said, "I'll bring some of my acquaintances who are here."

Dr. Ritchey invited others including Karl Harr, head of the Aerospace Industries Association, a public relations lobbying arm of the aerospace industry. We also invited Sister Fidelia, a nun;

Ken Delano, a priest who was interested in astronomy; Natalie; Earl; myself; John; John's wife; and a few others. Meanwhile, I raced to the apartment to pick up some cold cuts, and within half an hour, about twelve people had gathered at 907 Fifth Avenue. We had drinks for a while and began to relax from the strenuous meeting.

When we gathered for dinner, Dr. Ritchey surprised everyone by standing up, lifting his glass, and saying, "I'd like to give a toast to our host. I was sitting on the platform today, and I heard Earl Hubbard speak of the need for new worlds. At first I thought he was completely wrong, but I haven't been able to get it out of my head all afternoon. The more I think about it, the more I think he's right. Not only *can* we work to develop new worlds in space, but we *should*; we *must*. I'd like to drink a toast to the concept of taking the next step forward to build new worlds."

For the first time I sensed the excitement of creating our own ground—not standing on someone else's purpose. This toast unleashed an outpouring of high feeling. I responded with a toast to Dr. Ritchey, saying it was men like him that were providing mankind with the tools of transcendence. Sister Fidelia congratulated everyone on the magnificent possibilities for the future. Earl made a heroic toast to the universal age. Everyone became very excited, except the man hired as a public relations lobbyist for the aerospace industry: "The public will never buy this."

After dinner Sister Fidelia and I were still working on Karl Harr. He finally said, "Ladies, I give up! If people like you think it's important for the future of mankind, you must be right, and maybe the public will buy it." Of course, in his heart he hoped we were right, but he had been so hardened and probably wounded by the difficulty of "selling" space from a vested-interest point of view that he couldn't believe in our innocent motivation. It never occurred to him that people who weren't paid to build rockets or be astronauts would care. He couldn't understand that there are people whose motivations are for the common good, yet who aren't self-sacrificing.

Karl always looks to me like a Roman gladiator, exhausted,

with a headache, in an old gladiator's outfit. I walk into his office, full of hope and joy, and ask him, "How's it going?" and he always says, "Badly." He asks me how it's going, and I always say, "Well." Neither of us has succeeded.

The evening was a surprising success. Several days later, Dr. Ritchey called, wanting to know when we could do it again. He thought we lived like this every day! He never dreamed it was the work of a lifetime just to have achieved even this beginning. He said he'd like to give a dinner and have the same experience.

Of course, he believed deeply in what he was doing, but there's no particular joy in the aerospace industry. They haven't received the moral sanction of the public; they have no verification of what many intuit—that they've made a great contribution—and no one in the industry had affirmed the meaning of his act in relation to the whole of mankind

But Dr. Ritchey decided to give a dinner at the Wings Club a few weeks hence. He wanted all the same people to be there and a few more. John Whiteside said, "I'm going to invite General Joseph Bleymaier, who developed the Titan III rocket." John called the general in Los Angeles, and said, "General, there's a dinner I think you should attend." Bleymaier came without further question. At the party at the Wings Club, John said, "Barbara, your target is General Bleymaier." I asked why. "Because he's the man who could lead the first mission to new worlds."

Dr. Ritchey once again started a toast. The excitement spread, almost like a biochemical reaction. When transcendent hope is stated, people want to give toasts; one after the other arose. For mine, remembering my instructions from John, I turned to General Bleymaier, a handsome Texan, a retired air force general, and said, "General Bleymaier, do you think you can build communities in space?"

He looked up, and said, "Yup! We have the technology to live and work in space. The important thing is the *timing*. If John F. Kennedy had said we're going to the moon 'sometime,' and not, 'within this decade,' it wouldn't have happened."

So General Bleymaier suggested we set a time frame for the

first colony in space. After dinner, we invited most of the guests back to our apartment. I sat next to General Bleymaier, and said, "General, we'd like to form some kind of committee or group to bring these ideas into action. Would you help us?"

The general, not known for his loquaciousness, said, "Yup."

The idea of forming some kind of committee to rally the ideas and people for an open "new worlds future" percolated in our minds, as we tested the receptivity of audiences and groups throughout the country. Earl was the spokesman. He had a powerful eloquence. I edited speeches for him out of our breakfast dialogues and passages from the books. Then we took him to Dayton, Ohio, to speak before The Engineers Club. John set up meetings for him with the press, and arranged talk shows and interviews. But we had some difficulty. Earl saw himself as the embodiment of "the idea." We were the workers. His absolutist, perfectionist, elegantly tailored personality cut off the tender stirrings of new action that "the idea" stimulated. After Earl left, John and I were always picking up the pieces, seeing what people were capable of doing, assuaging hurt feelings. However, the movement began to be nurtured and to grow through this constant tending to people and the expressing of ideas in gentle interaction, starting from felt needs and proceeding outward to the larger goals. Earl's work life was not in the mission as ours was; his primary purpose was the creation of works of art, their projection into the world, and his *person* as the embodiment of a new idea and ideal.

A critical debacle occurred at the Apollo 13 launch in April 1970, when Earl, the children, Mademoiselle Baldet, Sister Fidelia, John, his wife, and other friends congregated at Cape Kennedy. Our purpose was to introduce Earl to the press, the astronauts, etc., so John organized a large dinner of press, NASA people, and friends. Earl was to give a speech. But John arrived drunk! His speech was blurred, and he was swaying, trying to be jovial, and then trying to introduce Earl. I practically died with humiliation. I whispered to Mademoiselle to take the children on a jaunt to see the gantries at night. We tried to cover up as best we could.

That night Earl said, "We're finished with him. He's no good."

I pondered it by myself, all night, alone. The next morning I called John's room, miles down Cocoa Beach from The Pines where we were staying. His exhausted, weak voice answered: "I love you."

"John," I said, "I love you, too, but if you ever want to see me again you'll stop drinking. If I ever see you take a drink, wherever we are, I'll leave the table, walk away, and you'll never see me again. I mean it. You're meant to do this mission; you're the only person who knows how to do it. You've got to free yourself from every obstacle, external and internal, and, for God's sake, *do it!*"

He kept mumbling, "I love you."

I said, "I expect to see you at dinner tonight at The Pines. Everyone will be there. But if you take one sip of alcohol, I'll leave."

He came and he didn't drink.

My hunger was tremendously nourished by the two dinners and meeting John. For the first time I sensed the step to new worlds actually might happen. There was a strange psychological connect/disconnect and reconnect when I knew I actually *meant* to do it. I'd already sensed the psychological process of evolving toward a new state of being, but when we started planning with the man who built the Titan III rocket—and he said yes, we can do it, and yes, he could do it, and we need a time frame—the reality of humankind's integration and birth took on a new dimension.

John began to introduce me to his associates. One day he took me to the Pentagon and dropped me off at various offices of his colleagues, saying, "Tell them about new worlds, Barbara," leaving me with some startled and uncomfortable officer at the other side of the desk. One man was Billy Greener, who subsequently became assistant secretary of defense for public affairs. I plunged right into the case for space now in terms of the human potential: It could convert weapons spending to life-oriented technologies; it could provide an opening frontier and a nonmilitary productive competition between us and our adversaries—as a transition to a peaceful world—it could provide employment, new methods of environmental protection, and a deeper sense of purpose for all. I told him we wanted to establish a United States initiative for an integrated earth-space program. We established a rapport. When I told him that John was retiring from the air force to "take on this mission," he shook his head in amazement: "Well, he's a wizard. Anything he's ever decided to do, he's done. If he thinks a new worlds' goal can be established, he's probably right."

In the book *The Need for New Worlds*, which I was still working on with Earl toward the beginning of 1970, we were outlining a case for a new national and global goal: new worlds on earth, new worlds in space. We saw that if we didn't start in our generation to build new capabilities in space, some dire possibilities would occur. We believed the goal to establish the first space community should be started in 1976, because time is not on the side of waiting. The finite resources on this earth are being used up. There'll be more people whose needs must be met. Remaining fossil fuels must be used both to meet immediate needs and to establish the foothold in the universe. Renewable resources of energy—solar, geothermal, wind, and so forth—must be quickly gained through proper use of nonrenewable resources, or we might run out of energy before we secure our opportunity for universal life. We're given a few decades of evolutionary grace.

I kept reexperiencing the birth experience, the transition from womb to world—the gasping for breath, the reaching out for life, the coordination of our internal systems. I could *feel* the irritation running through our—mankind's—nervous system. The common reach toward the universe was essential for harmonious cooperation on earth.

The first major response to the crises we faced came from The Club of Rome, formed in 1968 by a group of European industrialists and scientists. They laid down the gauntlet to the human race: You are in a finite world; limit growth or die! But the "limits to growth" perspective denies the human race a choiceful future. If followed, it would incarcerate us in a closed system of increasing controls and depletion of resources. It's not natural for evolution to stop at some point and aim at "balance." What *is* natural is synthesis and transcendence, the creation of new forms out of old systems. From the womb perspective of a finite, earth-bound species, they were right: cybernetics, genetics, astronautics appear unnatural. But from our point of view they were the natural necessities for the next development of life—a universal species.

Krafft Ehricke tells the story of the erudite "fetal scientist" who's a cell in the womb of a baby in the seventh month. He predicts that, from current growth rates, by the eighth month there'll be severe overcrowding and pollution; by the ninth month there'll be massive starvation, suffocation, revolutions; by the tenth month die-offs will occur in most of the poorer nations of the world, etc. The problem is, the fetal scientist knows nothing of the coming birth—and its "suddenness"—and it can't be predicted from the womb perspective. The "limits to growth" advocates are the erudite fetal scientists, extrapolating from the past—with no positive vision of the future.

Out of such thoughts as these and many more, we began to formulate a case for new action. This case offered so many options and benefits that we decided to form a group of diverse people who could develop the goal, "new worlds on earth, new worlds in space," and bring it into the public arena for discussion and action.

John was a great new factor in my life. He was trying to make something happen for *this* purpose and not for some other. I was always attaching this goal onto some other vehicle and being rejected, asking people to do something *they* didn't want to do.

We went to various friends and acquaintances, such as Dr. Ritchey, General Bleymaier, Sister Fidelia, Natalie, and others, and invited them to the first meeting at our home in Lakeville, Connecticut, in June of 1970, to found The Committee for the Future (TCFF). This was a historic meeting. In fact, we produced a charter, based on "the need for new worlds." It was penned by my daughter Stephanie in beautiful calligraphy, and signed by all the participating members of the conference:

The Lakeville Charter

Proclamation of the Purpose of The Committee for the Future

Earth-bound history has ended. Universal history has begun. Mankind has been born into an environment of immeasurable possibilities. We, The Committee for the Future, believe that the long-range goal for mankind should be to seek and settle new worlds. To survive and to realize the common aspirations of all people for a future of unlimited opportunity, this generation must begin now to find the means of converting the planets into life support systems for the race of man.

This option includes within it the basis for employment for all; the basis for a meaningful world union; the basis for uniting all who seek to know more of the Creative Intention; the basis for a meaningful education; an acceptable basis for excellence, morality, and fortitude; the basis for a welfare program for the future of mankind; and the proper employment of frustration as the force to forge the new frontier. A challenge of this magnitude can emancipate the genius of man. For all who claim that freedom means the opportunity to give your best, the effort to settle new worlds offers proof that mankind's survival depends on freedom, for we will need the best of every man to take mankind the next step.

We believe that the time to state the new goal is now. Awareness of the new option can transform this troubled world from a place of despair into a sphere of hope, aspiration, and joy.

Therefore, we have come together as citizens and members of mankind to develop the proposal for the United States of America to lead mankind to new worlds; to work to have the proposal promulgated as a national goal at the earliest possible date; and to rally men and women of good will to implement the new goal.

We, the undersigned, dedicate our efforts to secure for all men on earth a new hope, a new future, and the opportunity to participate in universal affairs.

John developed what we called "The Green Book" (because it had a green cover), which laid forth a strategy to bring this case into the public arena in time for a presidential candidate to carry the message in 1976, the bicentennial year. (The emphasis on the

United States was not nationalistic in intention; the goal is global. It simply appeared that the United States was in a position to take initiative in cooperation with all other peoples.)

John thought The Committee for the Future should be a "nonorganization," calling upon individuals of different fields to do what they could, where they were, when they could. But the climate of opinion in the early seventies wasn't favorable to this goal. We were out of fashion: The campuses were alive with protests; if you didn't have some issue of pain to put forward, it was hard to get a hearing.

This first year was a floundering search for what to do. George Van Valkenburg, one of our original founding members, a film producer in Los Angeles, came up with an extraordinary idea in the fall of 1970. He pointed out that two Saturn V rockets would be left over from the Apollo program. TCFF could initiate the first "citizen-sponsored lunar expedition," using surplus NASA hardware. It could pay for itself through the sale of lunar materials and the various television and story rights that would be involved. There could be a global subscription; people could subscribe either as they might to a great National Geographic expedition, or with some further interest in the development of space, which they could participate in later.

One of the factors that convinced me to undertake the citizens' mission was my father. I lunched with him after the founding of TCFF and described the difficulty of getting the new worlds' goal articulated and discussed. He agreed it was necessary to go into space; he knew it was where the future lay. He saw that the future of the human race depended on a broad arena of action, and he wasn't attracted at all by the back-to-nature movement.

But he said, "Philosophy will get you nowhere. Unless people feel they can own a piece of the new world, you'll never make it."

I said, "But people can't buy land on the moon; we can't sell anything. However, maybe we can find some way whereby people would buy a ticket for a journey that might occur for their children. If space colonization develops into an operative mode, and if there are new facilities for human life in space, these first subscribers to the citizens' mission would earn some access to the new adventure."

My father said he'd back me in this plan of research and development for what came to be known as "Project Harvest Moon." He gave me $25,000 to get started. His reservations about the fantastic scope of the action didn't stop him from helping. He had faith that great new things *could* happen. That's what I love most about him—that faith and his willingness to risk for it. His gift was of vital importance to me, not only because it was the first contribution to our first concrete effort, but because my love and admiration for my father was now able to express itself in such a way that he could participate with me. This was something worth working for, something worthy of doing your best for. The issue he had posed to us as children: "You'll all be spoiled brats because there'll be nothing worth working for," was one to which I had found an answer that he actually believed in.

Telling the story became *doing it!*

I had to step forward and carry a primary responsibility.

Late one Friday afternoon we went to see Werhner von Braun, the handsome, brilliant father of the Saturn V rocket. Just back from the dentist, he sat unsmiling, his jaw stiff with novocaine. John and I went into his office, sat down, and tried to sound matter-of-fact.

"Dr. von Braun," I said, "we understand there's an extra Saturn V rocket left over from the Apollo program. We'd like to use it for a citizen-sponsored lunar mission—to get the people involved. Do you think the rocket would be available? We could pay for it by a people's subscription, sale of moon rock, television and movie rights—it would be the first time individuals all over the world could do a transcendent act together."

For a moment he just looked at us in stunned silence. "Well, uh, Mrs. Hubbard—I, uh, don't know why not." A funny half-smile formed on his face, as the rest of his jaw held rigid with novocaine. "Naturally, though, the Saturn V is passé—obsolete technologically. Why not get the people interested in investing in Skylab B. They could grow big crystals in space."

I sighed. "Dr. von Braun, people don't want to grow crystals in space. They want to go to new worlds. Just to be part of that effort would stimulate millions—they'd buy subscriptions so their children might have a chance. We'd do experiments, testing the utility of the moon; searching for water; testing to see if things grow; installing a telescope to seek other life."

Von Braun nodded. "Maybe you're right. You know, I've spent my life trying to get to the moon. I can't see myself sitting here trying to persuade you not to try, too. I'll help."

He gave us a list of the top leaders of NASA and we went to see the space men of the age, one by one. The same story, the same question, the same response from Dale Myers, director of Manned Space Flight; Kurt Debus, director of Kennedy Space Center; Homer Newell, associate administrator for Science Applications; Robert Gilruth, director of the Johnson Space Flight Center. Then we went to see Christopher Kraft, deputy to Dr. Gilruth, in Houston. He met us with a smile, his extraterrestrial eyes gleaming with interest.

"Mrs. Hubbard, I've read your husband's book. This step into the universe is a religion and I'm a member of it."

I smiled back. "I know, and you're right. We're meant to be a universal species. The purpose of Harvest Moon is to give all those who feel this way the chance to say yes together. They'll instantly become a natural constituency for the future."

"I'll do whatever I can. Let me know."

We stopped at Dr. Gilruth's office next door, after leaving Christopher. "Dr. Gilruth," I said, "we have a way for the people to get involved," and John and I told him the story.

He turned to an aide, almost tearfully: "Why isn't NASA doing this?"

At Homer Newell's office in Washington, we once again outlined our idea. Newell, too, was with us all the way. "Do you realize," he said, "the benefit from satellites if they become operational—education, medical care—" He gave a beautiful description of earth's new, extended nervous system.

"Dr. Newell, if we could initiate a people's mission, possibly we could break down some nationalistic barriers that prevent the benefits from being applied."

Newell agreed. "The benefits should be applied for all mankind. We are one people."

"I know."

"I'll do whatever I can," he promised.

Our next stop was on Fifth Avenue, Harry Winston, Inc., where one can find the most expensive jewels in the United States. As we were carrying briefcases, suitcases, and papers, and looking slightly worn out, customers and salespeople stared at us on the way to some sequestered back showroom. We sat at a table covered with grey felt to show the jewels. An elegant jeweler entered and looked at us quizzically.

"Would you be interested in purchasing lunar rock," I asked, "to turn into jewels? This would be on sale to sponsor a nonprofit citizens' mission to the moon."

He looked startled for a moment, then said, "You know, Harry Winston's son would be very interested in this. He won a prize building model rockets. Could you get stones in various sizes? What's the texture like? Are they beautiful?"

"They're not beautiful in the ordinary world. It's the symbol. People stand in line for hours to see one. They put slivers of old rockets in their wallets. It would be a sign that humanity could touch worlds beyond earth. We've been told the mission could return several hundred pounds. Some would go to science, of course, but most to the people."

"Well, I think we'd probably need the whole load. What would it cost?"

"A few hundred million," I said casually.

He didn't even blink. "Comparing each lunar stone to a carat of medium-quality diamonds, that's a fair price."

From there we headed for UNICEF, with Richard Nolte,

former ambassador to the United Arab Republic, one of the founding members of The Committee for the Future. We had an appointment with the director, M. Labouisse, and John and I described Harvest Moon to him.

"Dr. Labouisse," I said, "if there's any profit beyond paying for the mission, we'd like to give it to UNICEF to benefit the children of the world. We want to make it absolutely clear that this mission is not for personal profit but for mankind's profit."

Labouisse was poised, urbane, unruffled. "Very interesting, very worthwhile, Mrs. Hubbard. But what would happen to our other sources of funding from the United Nations and our Christmas card sales? If we get this money, what would happen to our next appropriation?"

I was annoyed. "That seems to be a rather narrow perspective to take on this great step for the children of the world."

We left Labouisse and located Congressman Olin "Tiger" Teague, Democrat from Texas, chairman of the Subcommittee on Manned Space Flight, the most powerful congressman for NASA's budget, and the third-ranking Democrat in the House of Representatives. He was sitting wearily at his desk, which was piled high with papers, momentoes everywhere. Teague was portly, red-faced, kindly.

He shook his head and rested his head in his hands. "I've never seen it so bad. What's wrong—I can't understand why Congress won't back the space program. I know the people want it. But I know they have to have a chance to get into it."

"Congressman Teague, we have a suggestion to help." I told him, and suddenly he stood and took my hand.

"Barbara, you write a resolution asking Congress to request NASA to look at this idea and I'll introduce it into the House of Representatives."

Without delay I called on my cousin Arthur Borden, a lawyer, in his Park Avenue office. "Arthur, would you write a resolution requesting Congress to ask NASA to cooperate with The Committee for the Future to consider the feasibility of a citizens' lunar mission?" He smiled with amazement, but he did it, and we sent it to Teague, who introduced it into Congress immediately as House Resolution 979.

The Committee for the Future testified before Teague's subcommittee. We were a strangely incongruous group of citizens amidst the aerospace industry spokesman and NASA personnel. The purpose of the hearing was simply: the shuttle. General Bleymaier was wearing his Texas cowboy hat. Ira Einhorn, with his long hair, had on a stocking cap and a backpack; he was a former radical turned evolutionary. Sister Mary Fidelia was there in her nun's habit. Richard Nolte was always the sophisticated intellectual, smoking his pipe. Lee Kaminsky was a long-haired, former Marxist-Christian turned video artist. Paul Congdon, academic dean of Springfield College, Massachusetts, was there. We all testified on the theme that the space program is needed for the development of the human potential. After the hearing, one of the congressmen came over.

"Mrs. Hubbard, we're only the Subcommittee on Manned Space Flight. You're asking us to think about the whole world."

"Congressman, you can't discuss the importance of the step into space without discussing the development of the world. Why don't we have a meeting with the members of various committees concerned with different aspects of United States policy to examine the impact of a large space goal on the economy, welfare programs, foreign relations, tax trade-offs?"

He shook his head. "There's no way for us to do that. We have no way to get together as a whole. Why don't *you* call the meeting?"

My frustration was mounting rapidly. "But that would take me five years! I don't see how you can legislate, how you can make decisions, if you have no way to look at the impact of a major new option on the whole system."

"We can't," he said, looking helpless, and walked away.

Shortly thereafter, a reporter called us from Houston where he had overheard some astronauts talking about the project. (Several had volunteered to fly.) The next day headlines around the world screamed: "Wealthy Group from East Plans Mission to Moon!"

The NASA public relations people were queried, and without consulting us, they replied: "NASA cannot support a mission like this." Suddenly letters came from around the world, asking to subscribe to the mission. Then came an offer to appear on TV during Apollo 14, and we agreed to go. But just as the momentum rose to a new height, a letter from NASA's acting administrator, George Low, came, saying NASA couldn't permit the mission. John and I hastily arranged a meeting with him. When we arrived he was surrounded by aides, looking tense.

"Dr. Low," I said, "I realize that the mission might sound strange to you, but we wouldn't be going through all this back-breaking work if we didn't believe the space program is vital. Your program's being attacked. Funds are cut. Why not work with us to develop the concept? If it's not well-conceived, help us make it better."

"Mrs. Hubbard, I agree with you about the need. But, you see, the people would never tolerate an accident on a nonscientific mission."

"Dr. Low, we intend to perform scientific experiments that are life-oriented. The people would be hiring NASA to do the mission. Your safety standards would prevail. Of course we have to recognize that there'll be accidents—no great achievements were ever accomplished without some loss of life. NASA should face this. But I personally think it's *more* acceptable to risk lives on a people-sponsored scientific-cultural-social mission than on one doing pure scientific research alone."

Dr. Low listened, but shook his head. "You may be right. But another point: your cost figures are off."

"Well," I said, "we got them from the last director of Manned Space Flight. He said *yours* were unrealistic. You're loading all the R&D costs on the people. That's not fair."

An edge of irritation crept across his face. "The fact is, Mrs. Hubbard, even though I sympathize with you, you don't know what you're talking about!"

For a moment all I could do was stare coldly at him, with a

strange sense of pity. "My dear Dr. Low, I admire the genius of the men of NASA more than almost anything else in the world. But I'm telling you from the bottom of my heart, as a citizen, and as a person who would give her life for this cause, you're making a disastrously bad judgment in not cooperating with the people. I'm sorry—not for you, but for the world—because the American space program is vital to the future." I left him, feeling the hurt that had suddenly darkened the atmosphere.

After the unsuccessful encounter with Low, Congressman Teague invited us to his office on July 19, 1971, to meet with Rocco Petrone, director of Apollo Project; Dale Myers of Manned Space Flight; and Mr. Grubb, NASA legislative liaison.

Teague surveyed our group collectively. "I don't want anyone to waste any more energy on this project. John and Barbara, I'd like you to hear what Rocco has to say, and Rocco, I want you to listen to them. Anything you two can agree on, I'll support."

Rocco had a big, burly football-player's body, but a high voice. "Barbara, I never thought I'd have to say this, but we can't go to the moon after Apollo 17. The rocket teams are already being disbanded; the backup teams won't exist; industries are already shut down. It wouldn't be safe."

I tried to remain calm. "I appreciate that, Rocco, but if NASA had been willing to look at our proposal last year, when we first called on all the key people, it wouldn't be too late now."

However, expecting this response, we had an alternative plan prepared by space-scientist friends in Huntsville—a citizen-sponsored, near-earth orbit mission, to be called "Mankind One." Its purpose would be to broadcast the benefits of the space program and the cultural unity in diversity of mankind. Both Myers and Petrone said they could "live with that."

Congressman Teague agreed. "All right, Barbara, you go and rewrite the resolution. Get NASA to agree with you, and we're in business."

John and I rewrote the legislation, substituting "near-earth orbit" for the words "lunar mission," and resubmitted it to NASA.

But they refused to respond. I called them from time to time, until my patience wore out. I reached the point once of saying, "The mothers of the world are going to unite! This is our children's future. You have no right to deny us access to our rockets. They belong to *people*, not you!" They had no idea how to cope with me; I was becoming shrill.

My role isn't one of anger and protest, but the bureaucracy was forcing me to become negative. So I took a vow not to let any institution do that. Dealing with NASA was like working with a giant marshmallow—the further in you went, the more lost you became. They didn't directly oppose you; they just absorbed you in their enormous inertia. I sensed the oppression of the faceless tyranny of bureaucracy. The corporate decision of NASA as a government agency was less responsive than the decision of any of the individual members. This pattern of self-destructive decision making may be necessary, because the motivation of existing organizations aren't appropriate for the new age. Although many of the individuals of NASA are great men and women, the agency operates as an instrument of government policy. Their interpretation of what people want is *not* accurate in our age; citizens are *not* sufficiently involved in decision making; leaders do *not* know what people want. In many cases, they're behind the aspirations of the people; they're responding to a false picture of reality.

We continued exploring the idea of Harvest Moon in spite of NASA's rejection. John and I took a trip to England, the Soviet Union, and Yugoslavia. I was invited to appear on Independent Television News in England during Apollo 16; they had heard of the Harvest Moon project. When we arrived at the studio, I was delighted to discover they had constructed a model of the experimental package called FIELD-1—the growing experiment, the search for water, with a telescope on the roof of the building.

I had about three minutes on television—Astronaut Gordon was with me—and was asked very briefly about the Harvest Moon project. "We're in Britain to suggest a citizen-sponsored lunar expedition following the Apollo series. We want to know if anyone in

England would like to subscribe to such a mission, if it proves feasible?" They showed the model of FIELD. Instantly the phone lines into the studio jammed. When I finished, members of the staff at the television station wanted to know how they could buy subscription tickets.

I was also invited to be on a BBC interview. As I was waiting to go on the air, I encountered the ambassador from Bangladesh, a distinguished, urbane, elegantly dressed gentleman, who was also to be interviewed. I took the occasion to question him. "We've been criticized for supporting the space program because people are starving in Bangladesh. Do you think it's right or wrong for us to be promoting an experiment for an internationally cooperative space program?"

With firmness and strength of conviction, he said, "We *must* support such a program. We, in Bangladesh, have no chance for survival in the old way. Our problems are too great. We have too many people; our resources are depleted. Unless there are new technologies, new methods, and new ventures, which we can eventually participate in, we are doomed in Bangladesh."

We went to the Soviet Union to speak with Ella Massevitch, one of the leading women scientists in the National Academy of Sciences in the Soviet Union, as well as with the editor of *Novotny Press*. The Soviet Union depressed me deeply. We were required to stay at a tourist hotel, a large, ugly building in a style they call "Stalinesque Gothic." It was jammed with visitors for the May Day celebration. John and I were in rooms across from each other. We were required to leave our keys with a concierge. When I called him in the morning, I was asked what I wanted to speak to him about. Furthermore, when we tried to make telephone calls to set up appointments, we couldn't get through to the secretaries; we asked the help of the Intourist people. We made a call at 9:00 in the morning and were told to call back at noon; the secretary was out. We called back at noon and the secretary was still out; she would be back at 3:00. We called at 3:00 and the secretary was out again; she would be back at 5:00. We called at 5:00 and the office was closed. We had only three or four days in Moscow, and the frustration of being unable to contact anyone mounted. Then they assigned us an Intourist guide who said she'd translate when we met these people.

I said, "Thank you very much but they speak perfect English and it won't be necessary to have a translator."

She said, "Yes, it will."

While we were waiting for our appointments, we took a drive through Moscow. Passing the giant University of Moscow, I asked her, "Is there any student unrest in Moscow?"

"No, none at all," she said. "If they have a problem, they go to their superior and get it solved."

"Well," I said, "the situation is entirely different in the United States. Almost everyone is restless, students are restless, and so are retired people and women and blacks—almost everyone."

She nodded. "It's unfortunate in the West, with your corrupt system, the drugs, the crime, the pornography. No wonder they're restless."

"You're right, we have a serious breakdown. Tell me," I asked, "what's the goal of your society?"

She responded quickly. "Better light industry, better consumer goods."

Ah ha! I thought. *The toy culture!* "Wait till you get it," I said, "then you'll be faced with the same situation we are. Now you have a material goal, but when your society achieves it, you, too, will be seeking the next level. That's where we are—our society is breaking down because, once achieved, material sufficiency isn't adequate; you'll find that out soon."

She looked back at me, and said, "Well, we're not all *that* content."

She was intrigued by the idea that the discontent of the West was a prelude to something new. She forgot her role as spokesman for Communist ideology, and we began to talk directly. I asked her what she thought about the cosmonauts and the space program. She hadn't given it much thought. I told her it was part of the emancipation of the human potential. I asked her for their vision of the good person. She spoke of the "Soviet man." I said, "Does this Soviet man represent a model for everyone?"

"No," she said, "we're superior and it probably can't come about until other people are changed, other cultures are destroyed."

"This Soviet man, does he recognize that we're all members of one body? Moving toward universal development?"

She shook her head. "I don't know."

We began to talk around this "I don't know." She told me afterwards that it was the most interesting conversation she'd ever had. There was a real openness to discuss the future as soon as we got off ideological ground.

Later I had an unpleasant experience at the Intourist desk. I suspected that the Intourist people were lying to me about all these telephone calls. I was exhausted; throngs of visitors from North Vietnam, China, crowded around me. Suddenly I broke down, tears streaming down my cheeks. "I don't believe you—you're lying to me. I want to see these people and you're preventing it!" As I cried they stared at me with very cold eyes, except for one younger woman who gave me a handkerchief.

The next day I did get my appointment with the editor of *Novotny Press*. His first words were, "I understand you think we're liars." I had been reported on! I found the network of impossibility closing in on me. If I had had to stay in that society, I would indeed have become mad.

Ella Massevitch met us in her office at the National Academy of Science with two or three men. She was the major person there, an attractive woman, about my age. We told her of the Harvest Moon project, and she was immediately sympathetic—the only person I met in the Soviet Union of any high position with whom there was a personal rapport. She said, "If there's really an effort to do something for humanity and not for the United States to get ahead of the Soviet Union, I'd like to support it." The men with her said the idea was unrealistic and not practical. But she was sympathetic, and, I believe, would have added her weight to it if we'd been able to follow through with NASA.

We asked permission to postpone our departure one day to see the May Day celebrations. Even though there was free space in the hotel and passage on a flight the next day, the Intourist officials denied our request. Exasperated, I asked, "Why?"

"Because only a certain number of people are permitted in the Soviet Union from the outside at any one time—"

When we arrived at the airport, we tried to change our tickets to a later flight to avoid a long delay in Frankfurt, Germany. Even though there were seats available on the more convenient flight, our request again was denied. No tickets were permitted to be changed in Moscow, they told me. The petty network of impossibilities closed in again. Suddenly I shouted at the woman, "You're acting like sheep; you call yourself free? Don't accept this!" No one would talk to me. I sensed a circle of fear; everyone backed away. I felt the way I had at the Museum of Modern Art. There, hope was being assassinated by those who had grown to love death; in the Soviet Union hope was being assassinated by the denial of individual personality and freedom. When confronted with denial of human development, whether the Western version of decadence, or the Soviet version of repression, I experience a powerful driving force to break that bond.

As we pursued the Harvest Moon project, it became clear that effort alone would not suffice. We were moving against the current bureaucratic system—they were stronger than we. Also, on college campuses, the climate of opinion was not congenial to any new hopeful option. I was failing to communicate; Earl, who was usually invited as our spokesman, would make an eloquent plea for new worlds, but although a few students would be interested, in general, there was hostility.

Furthermore, an unexpected reaction was occurring in me. I first felt it in South Carolina in October 1970. As part of our effort to bring the new worlds ideas into the public arena, Henry Cauthen, manager of the Educational Television Station, had invited Earl to speak to a group of citizens in South Carolina for a whole day, presenting the ideas of new worlds. John had sought out Henry, who planned to produce a one-hour documentary from the day's conversation. I should have been delighted. Instead, misery set in.

As Earl was rehearsing and John was busily making arrangements for him, I found my spirits sinking, falling down a well with nothing to hold on to.

During the day, a TV team and Earl went from location to location. Tears were running down my face and I stood behind trees, hiding in embarrassment. I felt faint. Without disturbing Earl, I went to our room, locked myself in the bathroom, and began to cry even harder. With all my practice at emotional self-discipline, I couldn't handle this raging anger. I was shocked to discover that something inside me wanted to speak and would no longer remain silent while Earl spoke. That feeling was tearing me apart.

When Earl returned, triumphant after a long day during which he had been well-received by the people—good questions, good responses, etc.—he found me red-eyed and exhausted.

"Barbara, what in the world is wrong?" He tried to embrace me.

A frightful repulsion seared through my body. "I don't know, I don't know." I couldn't bring myself to tell him the truth; it was so unfair. He'd worked so hard. He thought he was pleasing me. He took me to dinner alone, holding my hand, mystified. "Earl, you did so well, so well," I said, and started to cry again.

Finally he "got" it. Sighing deeply, he said, "I know what it is. You want to do it yourself. The more I succeed, the worse you're going to feel." He was really distressed, since I was literally his only contact with the world. He didn't have a single friend otherwise, male or female.

"That's not true, not true," I said. "There's room for us both; there's room for *everyone* in this effort. But I can't be secondary to you anymore." It burst out. "I have to speak for myself."

All at once he turned against John and Harvest Moon. "You're a fool to be wasting your energy on ridiculous projects like that. I can't believe you'd trust John's advice over mine. Why, he's nothing but a cheap huckster. You should be working with my ideas and with me, not him."

"Earl, I've spent twenty years on words and images. I believe in them with all my heart. But in this age, without the ability to act on them, they're inert—no life. We need a citizens' movement for the future." We really disagreed. I understood the necessity for his work, but he didn't believe in the need for mine.

The combination of the need to speak, not to be the person who was holding the microphone, and the desire for concrete action was leading to a major change in me. This change was made manifest one day in February 1971. John and I had an appointment to see Alexander Butterfield, President Nixon's special assistant at the White House, to inform the president about Harvest Moon. We were driving to the airport from Lakeville; we were late; I was irritable; we arrived at Bradley Field and missed the plane; the airport was fogged in; we missed our appointment at the White House and spent a great deal of time together at the airport.

John said, "It's been gradually dawning—Earl can't lead. If we continue to put him forward as the leader, this whole thing will fail. He's an artist, but he can't work with people. He's not the leader. You are. You're the one who's been taking the initiative. You're the one who's taking the risks, communicating, making things happen. I think the reason I behaved so badly at Apollo 13 is because I unconsciously knew Earl couldn't do it. I loved you so much. I knew we were going to fail unless you recognized yourself."

This was exceedingly hard for me to accept. During my whole life, I had tried to help someone *else* manifest the feelings I had inside me. Now John was saying I had to step forward and carry a primary responsibility. Deep in my heart, though, I wanted to do exactly that. So I accepted his vision.

At every step in the development of my new personhood it was necessary for someone to reflect my own inner feeling to me—to verify it. As seven years before, Jonas had made it possible for me to see myself as a useful part of the evolutionary process, now, through John's eyes, I was able to see myself as a primary factor in the action. I don't believe I could have seen myself the first or the second time without help.

---

*I wanted to do this
extraordinary thing.*

The next major step occurred at Southern Illinois University, where we held a conference in May 1971—"Mankind in the Universe"—the culmination of several small conferences we had had in Lakeville with students from Southern Illinois University. John's son was in college there; many of the young people we knew were from SIU.

Earl was to address the student body in the Arena, which was like a prize-fighting ring with thousands of seats around it. He gave one of his set speeches, which he had asked me to edit for him. Dressed in dark blue suit, white shirt, red tie—very elegant, he was totally out of phase with the style of the students and faculty in blue jeans, the casual garb of protest. His speech didn't go over. It was a pure call for heroism in the age of the antihero. He had his own form of courage—to stand, completely different, and expose himself to the hostility of those he would serve without accommodating one iota.

Subsequently we had several small meetings in which I spoke to classes. On one occasion, I proposed the idea that there was a new way to meet the hierarchy of human needs. I was trying to shape the humanistic argument for the space program. However, I was attacked by students; one said, "Why do you want to continue 25,000 years of failure?" This was the time of the radical rejection of human society by certain elements of our culture.

An older man, Herbert Marshall, professor of drama, rose in towering wrath: "You would have kept us in the caves! You wouldn't even have dared step into the light."

I went on to say, in a gentle way, that man had not failed, that we were a young species at a point of transition. It was *possible*, for the first time, to overcome those terrible lacks that had forced us into bad behavior, such as poverty, disease, ignorance. Our new tools might transform the species on earth as well as liberate it for new life in the universe. I heard one student snicker at me. I took courage, stared him in the eye, and said, "Did I hear you snicker?" The long-haired, blue-jeaned, white-faced twenty-five- or twenty-six-year-old, perennial-student type sank in his seat. "How dare you snicker at mankind! How dare you snicker at the effort of the past! Do you have any idea of the effort that went into the development of the human species? The suffering, the anguish of the people working day in and day out to eat, to survive, to keep their children alive? You're sitting in this heated building in an affluent society, snickering at the past!" I rose to defend humanity against this arrogance. The nights in Lakeville, listening to Beethoven, looking at the paintings, meditating joyfully on the goodness of the human struggle, strengthened me to speak in total love. But I left the platform feeling a failure. My desire had been to create consensus and affirmation. Instead I had instigated dissention. Earl's speech was out of context in its purity, and my efforts had aroused heated argument, rather than affirmation.

The next morning Professor Tom Turner asked John and me to sit with him on the stage. In the audience were several hundred people who had attended the various seminars and activities of the "Mankind in the Universe" conference. Earl was there, too. Tom, who looks like a soft, comfortable dolphin—round, gentle, and sweet, but intelligent—started out mildly by saying that Buckminster Fuller had been talking for some time about the importance of women's leadership for the new age.

"Therefore," said Tom, "we would like to make a recommendation: that Barbara Marx Hubbard run for the nomination for the presidency of the United States on the Democratic ticket. Her role would be to carry the options for the future into the public arena. She can state the alternatives and new possibilities better than any other candidate." He called on the assembled group to pass a resolution from SIU.

I was stunned. The surprising thing was that I felt innately natural, happy—that it was a good idea. The conviction of the rightness of "new worlds on earth, new worlds in space" was so deep inside me that when Tom said it, I stood without hesitating and made an acceptance speech. "It's true women *do* have a new role to play. As we lessen our role in reproducing the species, we must strengthen our role in the maturing of the species; love, co-operation, and nurturing qualities, combined with intellect are needed." Suddenly I noticed Earl's face staring at me. He was in anguish. I avoided his eyes; I didn't want to be stopped. By the time I finished, the hunger was tremendously excited by the possibility of large-scale, mainstream action. Unaccountably, I wanted to do this extraordinary, unprecedented thing.

Many people got up to second the nomination. Various constructive suggestions were made—it would provide new international initiatives, a new, nonpolitical approach to the future, etc. The last person to speak was Earl. He was sitting along the aisle and began to pace up and down like a prisoner. "I think this is a very *bad* recommendation," he said. "The idea must *not* be associated with one person, certainly not with *my wife*! It could be ruined. What we need is for Southern Illinois University to take it on. You people, professors and students, should develop the ideas and bring them into the political arena."

He tried to make a case for the university—which was totally unrealistic, since large state institutions don't take anything like that "on." They couldn't even agree on a president of the university —the administration was in disarray, etc. But I understood his anguish, and felt it with him. Still, I was angry that he would cut me down like that.

We broke for lunch. The resolution was written and read as soon as we reconvened. It said: We propose that Barbara Marx Hubbard carry the positive options for the future into the public arena, seeking the Democratic nomination for president of the United States. The vote occurred—everyone was affirmative, except for two: Earl Hubbard and a young man, whose name I don't remember, brought by Sister Fidelia.

Later that afternoon I received a message that Buckminster Fuller wanted to see me. Naturally Earl came along. Bucky was sitting in his office, surrounded by his books, plaques, pictures—memorabilia of a lifetime. I sensed the tremendous contribution he had made to humanity. The first thing he said was, "Well, young lady, I hear you've been nominated for the presidency."

He spoke laughingly and I laughingly said yes. I wanted to discuss it with him, but I wasn't given the chance to say a word. Earl broke in, asserting his vision of the importance of space. Fuller became irritated and asked Earl whether he had read his books: "You know, the ideas you're promoting I've been writing about for years." Earl said no, he hadn't read them. Fuller became outraged, and said, in essence, How dare you set foot on my campus if you haven't even read my books!

Later that night, in our bedroom, Earl couldn't sleep. He was pacing the floor in the middle of the night and woke me. "Barbara, I beg you not to accept this nomination—it would destroy me. I could never hold my head up again with my children. I could never hold my head up again with my family, or with my peers."

I weighed my decision carefully. My innermost desire was thrilled and wanted to try. The voice that guided me intuitively from time to time urged me onward. But my reason asserted it was an incredible act that might do what Earl said—diminish the viability of the new worlds' goals. But the main question was, Is it *right* to hurt Earl to satisfy what might be merely an ego need of mine? Dare I risk his well-being because I wanted to do this extraordinary thing? I meditated for hours, and he paced the floor. We didn't speak. Finally the decision rose to my consciousness: I couldn't hurt him to satisfy myself. My "signal" on running for the presidency was not authoritative or clear enough to risk mortally wounding him.

"Earl," I said softly, breaking the tense silence, "I promise not to run for the presidency." It sounded strange. The sentence hung in the air like a bird I'd never seen before.

He stopped pacing; his body relaxed. "Thank you, Barbara. Do you promise never to run?"

"No, Earl, I can't promise that."

The following morning I had to face John. He wanted me to do it. He thought we had a chance to gather the energy of discontent and disenfranchisement—those who liked neither Nixon nor the familiar Democrats. "John, I've decided not to do it. We have very little chance, and it would hurt Earl."

He shook his head. "You're wrong, Barbara. You've made the wrong decision. It could make all the difference." He walked away from me, still shaking his head.

A few days later I joined my father for lunch, stopping first in his office at 200 Fifth Avenue. He sat behind his desk, puffing the familiar cigar, leaning back in his large chair, beaming at me. "Well, Barbara, how are you? What's been going on?"

"Dad, I've been asked to run for the nomination for the presidency on the Democratic ticket." I pulled the SIU resolution out of my purse and handed it to him across the desk.

He read slowly, looked up, and said matter-of-factly, "You ought to do it. It's a good idea. Run on both tickets, like Eisenhower did. You're not a politician. Call it the Unity party."

Strategies started to crop up in his mind like daisies in spring. I was amazed at his acceptance of this idea. But it's been consistent with my father—when a great concept took root in me, such as the citizen-sponsored space mission, and running for the presidency, he, of all my family, instantly understood it and wanted to support it.

The Unity party—it echoed in my ears. Certainly *something* was needed, a new way to bring people together. My "total commitment" had been triggered by the dissention and self-disgust after the 1969 lunar landing. In 1972 nothing had improved. Groups didn't trust each other; no one really knew what anyone else thought; communities, disciplines, generations, races, religions were fragmented. Yet we're one body. We have the ability to "make it." What's wrong? Even when we expressed the new worlds' goals, people who agreed would say, "I get it, but the other fellow won't." Then we'd go to the "other fellow" and find he got it but expressed the same misjudgment about someone else. The problem was attitudes. There was no method, no process, for people to find out what others thought. Society had separated us from each other unnaturally. The result was disintegration—social disease.

---

*I began one of the most
fascinating journeys of my life.*

One day John was fiddling with the linear examination: if we have a large space goal, what would be the impact on the economy, welfare, international relations, etc.—something was always left out. In a flash of insight he turned the linear examination into a wheel. He put all the functional areas of any social body in the inner circle of the wheel like pieces of a pie facing each other— production, environment, technology, social needs, other regions of the world, government—with a coordinating hub in the center where each sector could match needs and resources and compare each other's goals. He added a satellite at the growing edge of the circle called nature of humankind. The "new potentials" were also put at the "growing edge" of the wheel: the biological revolution, new powers in the physical sciences, new capacities in the information sciences, extraterrestrial development, political-economic theory. The arts were represented by a dotted line—the skin around the wheel; they were the synthesizers and motivators. Without the arts, people can't see themselves struggling to be whole, can't visualize where they want to be. Finally, there was a far-out satellite, nonverified phenomena—the intuitive, mystical, psychic experiences of the human race. It looked as though we had a social process to bring the body together as a whole. Seeing the first picture of it, I thought it looked just like a cell!

John said there should be television in every section, a reality factor and a security blanket, with a central, open "mission control" where anyone could see everything at once.

"Just like you did for the space program," I said. "We'll be able to see ourselves in all our separate parts as one organism—that's great!"

"Yes, and we can broadcast live and have people call in," John added.

"My God!" I said. "You're giving us a social nervous system!" I was thrilled. I *knew* it was right. We decided to use the wheel format for the next conference at SIU—May 1972.

John and I then "hit the road" for one of the most fascinating journeys of my life. Our purpose was to get the broadest possible cross section of people who didn't agree with each other to form task forces in each sector and ask them to look at their own felt needs in light of the growing capacities of society as a whole. During the process they would have the chance to merge gradually with corollary but apparently conflicting groups—such as environmentalists with technologists—to check for common goals. Finally we would remove all the "walls," and the group would meet as one body. The growing edge would report on the body's new opportunities, and the conflicts would be discussed in the open. The attempt would be to solve one group's needs without hurting someone else: a new game, with new rules—how can *everyone* benefit?

The timing was right. Almost everyone we invited said yes. Labor had reached the point where, if it demanded more benefits, it would seriously jeopardize the industry and the economy upon which it was dependent. Business couldn't continue to maximize profits at the expense of an environment of which it was a part. Environmentalists were advocating stringent controls, which were affecting the economy upon which people were dependent for survival. Technologists couldn't continue to advocate solutions that damaged the biosphere. Human services recognized that after thirty years of welfare and an estimated trillion dollars' expenditure, there was still no success in providing genuine well-being to those who are excluded.

We wrote an article for Ed Cornish's *Futurist* and as a joke named the process SYNCON—an acronym for *synergistic con-*

vergence. It means the coming together of all vital elements of the social body to discover their functional relationships to each other and to the whole: Together the whole is greater than the sum of its parts; therefore, each participating member becomes "greater" through inclusion in the whole.

The year of the first SYNCON—1972—was the beginning of the end of my past family life. In 1970–71, although I travelled a good deal, my home base was definitely Lakeville. But with the SIU SYNCON my physical base shifted to constant travel, so that 1972 was the year the fabric ripped apart. Suzanne and Stephanie were away at school. They sympathized with me; much as they loved and admired their father, they knew I had to be free to grow—they wanted to do just that themselves. I had a long phone conversation with Suzanne. "Mummy, we're with you all the way," she said. "You're *right* to do what you're doing. You *must!*" She gave me enormous moral courage. Fortunately Alexandra, Wade, and Lloyd led a normal, happy life with Mademoiselle Baldet. She was able to act as a living link between them and me. They trusted her deeply. She loved both me and them; spiritually, she joined me in my task while physically, day by day, she cared for them. I telephoned them almost daily—to find out what was going on in their lives. Once I could get beyond the "fine, thank you" stage of the conversation, they reported the major events—seeing deer, the movies, skiing. We never lost connection with each other. With Earl, though, it was far more painful. His personality demanded total dedication from me and center stage with others. His pain broke my heart, but there was nothing I could do. For even as he awed people with his brilliance, he pushed them away with his demand for perfection. We couldn't get anything started with him at the core.

SYNCON eve, John was already at Southern Illinois. I was to fly there the next day with the participants from New York. About 250 people were expected. I was in Lakeville, packing, saying goodbye to the children and to Earl, who had decided not to come, even though I had invited him, when the phone rang. It was Stanley Reese, suddenly appearing from out of my past. My sister Patricia, who had married Daniel Ellsberg, had told me that when they were trying to raise funds for Dan's defense, Stanley had offered to head up the fund-raising effort. Patricia had met him in his elegant house in San Francisco—not having seen him since she was twelve, when he and I were dating. She confided in me that he had sent his best regards—and more. He had earned a fortune, had married a wealthy girl whose father was a powerful, cultivated person. Patricia said he couldn't be recognized as the young man I had brought to Scarsdale. I was profoundly moved to hear his voice. "Where are you?" I asked.

"I'm in New York, waiting to see you. I want to see you tonight."

"But I'm getting ready to go to Carbondale. I don't see how I can. I'll see you when I return."

"No." He insisted. "I must see you now. I'll be flying to England tomorrow." His accent had changed from Philadelphia Southside to a combination British-Mexican, where he had earned a fortune in mining.

I was irresistibly compelled to see what he was like. "All right. I'll meet you in the lobby of the Algonquin. We can talk there. I'll spend the night at Aunt Rose's."

Mademoiselle Baldet drove me the two-and-a-half hours to the city. It was about eleven o'clock when I entered the lobby of the comfortable, old Algonquin, squinting my near-sighted eyes. There he was—elegant, transformed, in a turtle-neck sweater, so handsome, drinking champagne. I sat beside him, speechless. We just looked into each other's eyes—nothing ever really dies that once was felt deeply.

"What does it feel like?" I asked. "You've achieved everything you wanted—wealth, beauty, high position. Has it been worth it? Does it feel satisfying?"

He shook his head. "No," he said. "It's worth nothing. It has no purpose—I have no purpose."

"Let me share with you what I've learned. Let me tell you what's happened to me. I've found a way—"

He raised his hand to silence me. "I don't want to hear it yet," he said. "I want to savor this moment a little longer. You can tell me later."

"I must tell you now." But he wouldn't let me talk. I felt so close to the threshold of communication. But there was and is something in him that wants to possess before becoming open. That night I slept a few restless hours at Aunt Rose's apartment, feeling the desire to bind the past and the present into one as I headed to the new—the future, the first SYNCON at SIU.

When I arrived at Southern Illinois University I found John in the student ballroom. I was thrilled—the students had built a cosmic wheel! In the center was the coordinating hub, with a little spiral staircase that went up to a balcony, where anyone could look down upon the body as a whole. The stage was being set for a new experience, one that had urged me forward and tantalized me from the very beginning—the hunger for wholeness and transcendence. In each sector of the wheel were a TV camera and a monitor so participants could both see what was happening in the other sectors and be recorded themselves. The internal nervous system was ready to operate.

The task forces worked all that first day till the afternoon of the second, preparing their first summaries of goals, needs, and resources. Occasionally John, who "produced" the event, would flash a "focus item" over the internal television system, such as Lazar Mojsov, United Nations ambassador from Yugoslavia, addressing the need for cooperative technological exchange between the developing and developed worlds. Each of these talks was given from the site of the functional task forces, to symbolize that there's no audience, no speaker, everyone is a participant, each sector is vital to the whole.

Every evening before dinner we presented the "New Worlds Evening News," a newscast in a format like "CBS Evening News," taking the highlights of the day's SYNCON activities, adding news highlights of the outside world. The contrast was obvious: Most of the news from the regular mass media was of catastrophe, breakdown, and disagreement. The news from the SYNCON was of the struggle to find linkages and to match needs and resources. There were arguments, but they tended toward seeking agreement, rather than stressing differences. These evening newscasts were played during the cocktail hour; people wanted to see them over and over again.

On Saturday morning the "walls" came down. Participants gathered in the wheel, in their merged groups. Questions went around the wheel, each group trying to gain the assistance of the other in handling some problem. I could *feel* the social body trying to adjust and coordinate itself as one, each element trying to avoid injuring another. It was the *same* feeling when I sensed myself part of the social body trying to coordinate on the hill in Lakeville There were experts in each part, but none in the coming together of the whole body. Thus we experienced a new kind of equality. We were in that instant a microcosm of the macrocosm; we were all in it together, learning something new.

People felt increasingly united by some bond deeper than words could express. A psychological field of force was drawing them closer and closer. They didn't want the "SYNCONNING" to stop. People of enormous diversity had grown attached to each other. John Yardley, the space scientist, Carl Madden, the establishment economist, and Ira Einhorn, the radical evolutionary, drove away in a convertible, with Ira Einhorn's long hair whipping into Carl Madden's face. There was a desire to "do it again"; some wanted to hold one where they lived. As the body of people were forced to separate, they wanted to hold the links together in some way.

For the hunger of Eve, this was a feast, a social manifestation of the birth experience of oneness. We had created a model of social relations that represented mankind as a whole, with its functional systems present—with a process for each group to discover how it could best fit and grow in the whole.

The idea of "supra-sex" suddenly occurred to me. The excitement of connecting, of fusing differences, has a sexual overtone; however, the emphasis isn't on personal union, but rather a transpersonal, multiple creation, through the fusing of ideas. As our role in reproducing the species biologically diminishes, our action to produce our future through the coalescing of goals and aspirations will increase. The attraction that drew us together here was no more idealistic than sex. It was an innate desire for social intercourse. In this state of being, we naturally felt related to all life and wanted to *act* in concert with others. The dichotomy between selfish and selfless diminished. Sensing ourselves as one body, feeling the joy of the connecting act, also opened and sensitized us to spiritual awareness; in some sense the entire act was infused with the *reality* of religion, the root meaning of which is *re-ligare*, to bind back again and make whole.

After the SYNCON, on June 14 we met Astronaut Edgar Mitchell at the Gotham Hotel, where we had taken a small suite. He had been a SYNCON participant. It was Saturday morning. John had gone to repark the car, and I was alone in the apartment when Ed rang the doorbell. As he entered the room, trailing clouds of glory of his experience, I began to laugh. "Ed, what in the world brings a former housewife from Lakeville and a former astronaut together at the Gotham Hotel to talk about the unity of mankind?"

Ed said, "Barbara, all I know is that I'm operating under orders. I've lost all fear. I've come to believe that there are no accidents. Just when I think all is lost I put my foot down over an abyss—and something comes up to hit it, just in time."

John returned, and Ed described to us his plans for The Institute of Noetic Sciences. His purpose is to demonstrate that psychic phenomena—the mind force, healing, telepathy, clairvoyance, psychokinesis, astral travel, consciousness itself—are "real" phenomena and can be studied scientifically. I asked him how this happened to him—a trained physicist. He had had an experience similar to mine. "When I was on the moon," he said, "I looked at earth—I could feel its anguish, its struggle—and I fell in love with humanity as a whole."

We established a linkage on a deep level. I sensed a new element fitting perfectly into my own being, enlarging me by the extent of his being, and hopefully my being enlarging his.

But in spite of these cases of individual empathy, it became apparent that even at the highest level of development, various sectors of the body of mankind don't recognize the validity of the other sectors. It may be that the recognition will come from the so-called common man, who doesn't have a vested interest in expertise in any of the sectors.

When we met Dr. Ben Schloss and were discussing the study of the aging process, I asked him what he thought about psychic phenomena. He said, "It doesn't exist."

"How can you be so dogmatic?" I asked. "Throughout history there have been reports of healings, of telepathy, of intuitive experiences, beyond the ordinary."

He shook his head, dismissing it. "I can *prove* to you that it doesn't exist."

When I asked Ed Mitchell what he thought about physical immortality, he said, "It's of no significance. Our consciousness will live on without our bodies."

"How do you know that?" I asked. He had no more proof of that than Schloss had that there were no psychic phenomena.

Edgar Mitchell, the physicist, and Ben Schloss, the biologist, both breaking frontiers, have views that *exclude* the other. It's as if the young mankind has developed an allergy to its various parts. One side of the body gets hives at the thought of the other. The cosmic child has colic! The fact is, brilliant as any individual may be, no one knows *all* the laws of the universe. It's arrogant for a young species like humankind, barely gaining access to knowledge and to self-awareness, to make dogmatic pronouncements on the nature of the universe.

I was totally absorbed in this new action, but I kept returning to Lakeville for the weekends to be with the children. I don't know when it dawned on me that I had separated from Earl. It wasn't a conscious act; it was simply that I was involved totally in a new life.

For many months I didn't write in my journal. It represented to me the quest. Now that the emphasis was on realization through action, the need to write lessened. It wasn't until 1973 that I wrote:

> Since I last really wrote in my journal, Earl and I have separated. I can only explain it in terms of different "karma" or destiny. I was literally commanded to go forth. John

Whiteside, the first man who has really loved me for what I want to become, revealed to me that my role was not to remain a secondary function to serve the liberation of Earl's potential.

Earl adamantly and steadfastly remained true to his own destiny, which is to conceive in word and image the next step of the creative intention. He wanted me to serve him in his purpose, and I simply no longer could. Every fibre of my being called out for independent action.

---

*This is the closest I ever came
to touching the Tree of Life.*

John, in one of his altered states of action, decided we should have a meeting in Tucson directly after the SYNCON with Paul Henshaw, the biologist, as our host. We invited Krafft Ehricke, space scientist; John Yardley, vice-president of McDonnell Douglass; and Florence Hetzler, philosopher. We met in John Yardley's motel room.

When Krafft arrived I asked him about his concept—the technological-industrial basis for the next step in evolution. He's a silver-haired German, of the original rocket-building Penemunde group that left Germany—one of the greatest, little-known geniuses on planet earth. Sitting on the foot of the bed—his cheeks flushed, his eyes alive, his hands gesturing—he talked about the entire process of creation. He felt it—like I did; and I loved him as he talked about the "Extraterrestrial Imperative."

During the first crisis the single cells, having depleted the organic compounds synthesized during the formation of earth, responded with the "biotechnical accomplishment of photosynthesis," gaining extraterrestrial sources of energy. However, the process of photosynthesis produced a "waste"—oxygen, which was poisonous to single-celled life and prompted the emergence of multicellular organisms. Now, facing the second great crisis of limited fossil fuels and the danger of increased industrialization to the fragile biosphere, we need to build the "androsphere," humanity's sphere, creating an integrated, indivisible environment of earth and space. Weightlessness, vacuum, continuous solar energy, lunar and asteroidal materials, and the *lack* of a biosphere make outer space a better place than earth for the next phase of industry. The second great crisis is thus another evolutionary driver, pressing us forward to develop an "open-world" system, the material basis for the next step in human development, a step that will also provide the basis for immeasurable development of the human mind and spirit. Krafft was describing the technology of mankind's birth into the universe!

Krafft had to leave at the end of the day to return to California. We embraced—this discussion was one of the most exciting of my life.

As John Whiteside went to the flip chart on the headboard of the bed, everyone suddenly burst out laughing at the incongruity of our seriousness and the setting. After we settled down he laid out a strategy, first outlined in the "Green Book," for achieving a public mandate to call for the goals of "new worlds on earth, new worlds in space," or the building of the "androsphere." We planned to *act out* the philosophy Krafft had abstractly presented. We were responding to "evolutionary drivers." We were evolving as we sat in the motel!

Conversation flowed rapidly from person to person, like music tempo increasing. We were gaining access to each other's minds, knowledge, and very being. We were fusing! Every nerve and cell in my body awakened, and I had to leave the group. I rushed out to the patio near the pool and began to do some yoga exercises to release the pressure. In fact, I was standing on my head when John Yardley joined me, and in that comic position we conversed about our personal intuition of universal life.

He wanted to record our conversations and had brought four different tape recorders; each malfunctioned. I had experienced the same curious phenomenon while I was dictating *The Hunger of Eve*. Andrija Puharich writes in his book on Uri Geller that when the voices of a group, which they called "Spectrum" and experienced as extraterrestrials, were recorded on their tape, it erased mysteriously. Similarly, Laurens van der Post, in his biography of Carl Jung, reports that he was preparing to interview Jung for the BBC, when Jung said, "I warn you, things of this sort hate me. You might think they are inanimate but in my regard I tell you they're highly animate and even active and hostile . . ." (Van Der Post: *Jung and the Story of Our Time*). If it's true that the extended nervous system of the body of mankind is its media, perhaps the media is literally blocking out signals of the new voices; their vibrations may overload the existing electronic system. I don't like to be esoteric, but I *have* experienced kinesthetically that the nervous system of the body of mankind is our electronic media. If that's so, the electronic nervous system is as alive on a planetary scale as my nervous system is in my own body.

Throughout the meeting at Tucson, I had the feeling of parts of the body awakening, linking, "turning on and tuning in" to each other until the whole earth became alive, recognizing itself as one and sensing that it was a *good one*—a feeling of love of our larger self: the body of humankind. At that instant I had felt myself to be both parent *and* child. I loved the whole body from the perspective of a mature, parental culture. I "forgave" us our "sins," much as a mother "forgives" the infantile behavior of the newborn child. From the cosmic perspective, we *are* infantile, unable to coordinate, fighting ourselves, unaware of who we are, where we came from, or what we may grow up to be. We are "dangerous," capable of causing our own destruction, perhaps even affecting our portion of the universe. That's the danger of the Tree of Life. Like that of a newborn child, our condition is serious, but the potential for survival seems to be there. On the other hand, feeling myself to be part of the body, an infant, too, with the same irritability, self-centeredness, and faults, I forgave *myself* my sins, and had compassion upon myself as well as all others. I call this experience "the synergizing earth." I *know* it will happen because in some sense it already *is* happening and *has* partially happened to me and others. The real-time experience I expect will be totally overwhelming—a genuine joy on earth, goodwill to all.

My experience at Tucson is the closest I ever came to touching the Tree of Life—of participating consciously in the evolutionary process. It felt so good, so natural, so right.

We were already cooperating . . .
we were one.

John was developing the concept of the "new media." The use of television at the SIU SYNCON was a first prototype. He was applying what he had learned through live coverage of the space program to the live coverage of human interaction and development. He became convinced with almost inexplicable certainty that we should purchase our own television system especially designed to make a new model for the communication of human convergence, creation, agreement, and synergy. I would never have conceived of this myself. I was acting under sheer faith in his ability to envision a new communication system. I did know, from experience, that the media, as it's now operating, is one of the blocks to evolution. Therefore, I decided to invest a substantial sum to purchase a specially designed television system.

It was an act of faith; however, I had always felt the money I inherited should have some purpose other than making myself and my children comfortable. My father was opposed to my using the money he'd given me for my own "work." He thought of it as a "charity." From his perspective, I was like a young lion cub giving away the hunt that had been brought in by the father lion. I was squandering the material security he had so laboriously built up. From my point of view it was an investment in the future, which might benefit all children. I understand his perspective. One needs to keep balanced in these areas—money is very difficult to make and too easy to give away—but I thought it was proper to use some of my inheritance to develop a model for a new communications system that might have a chance of furthering mankind toward universal life.

So we ordered the new equipment: "SYNCONsole," which is a central board very much like mission control at Houston, where you can see all the sectors at once. Television cameras and monitors for every sector of the wheel were purchased. I thought it might help the interconnecting of people, so we could share the experience.

We tested the SYNCON in a variety of places to see if the SIU event were a lucky accident or if the process were repeatable. We tried it twice in Los Angeles, once with brilliant types like Ray Bradbury and Jean Houston, once in the inner-city Watts area with black and Mexican-American gang leaders as the major participants—also in Huntsville, Alabama; Knoxville, Tennessee; and Washington, D. C. during the Watergate crisis. It worked every time. People connected. One of the most interesting efforts was in Jamaica.

I met a young information officer from Jamaica, Peter Bentley, during a talk I gave in Huntsville. In the middle of one of my conversations, Peter interrupted abruptly, saying, "Barbara, how fast can you get to Jamaica?"

I was astonished. "What do you mean?"

"A group has been asked by the prime minister of Jamaica, Michael Manley, to present a proposal for a developmental plan for the whole nation that would include people's participation in the planning process—SYNCON might be the method."

I asked him to discuss it with John and me at the Washington SYNCON the following week. It had never occurred to us to go to Jamaica, but he was persuasive and also offered to lend us a place to stay in Ocho Rios for a few days. Exhausted from the effort of the Inner-City and the Washington SYNCONs, we accepted Peter's invitation and spent three days at Ocho Rios, a magnificent site on the ocean. It was like the few moments at Eden Rock many years before. I was divinely happy, cut off from the pressures of this work we'd undertaken, for a few moments living in luxury and ease. I thought if peace and beauty were the aim of humans, we would never have left the Garden of Eden, for surely this was like the garden.

Peter made an appointment for us with Dr. Gladstone Bonnick, director of national planning. He's a tall, slim, elegant black man. I felt nervous entering his office, because of my ignorance of the Jamaican situation. I described SYNCON and Dr. Bonnick "got it" immediately. He said the prime minister had wanted a "consultative department" for all different groups to consult with him before he made up his program. It didn't work because he found himself the target of every special interest. Manley was asking for a process whereby these special interest groups could interact with *each other* before coming to him. Bonnick saw SYNCON as such a process. He felt it shouldn't be sponsored by the government because the opposition would immediately suspect it. He suggested we see Lester Kirkcaldy, head of the National Council of Jamaican Organizations, as the sponsor.

That day we met Lester at lunch on a beautiful terrace restaurant blown by the soft breezes of Jamaica. Lester is a black Scotsman with ancestors from the town called Kirkcaldy—a tall, dark man, with wide eyes and a strange, large nose. I looked into his eyes and almost immediately felt a rapport with him. He had brought together seventy-three organizations to cooperate in the development of the country but lacked a process. His motivation seemed spiritual. He said, "In every person there's a potential wanting to come out, but it's thwarted due to environment or institutions. Maybe SYNCON can help bring it out."

I said, "Lester, we must be scooped out of the same genetic material," as Jonas had said to me years earlier.

We laughed and decided to cooperate. We didn't even decide; we were already cooperating—we were already one. John tells me I'm overly naive and optimistic when meeting people who appear to be soulmates, but I can't get over the joy of it after all my young adult years of noncommunication. It's a thrilling experience. I told

Lester I felt closer to him than some people I'd lived next to my whole life, even some members of my own family, even though he was a person with a totally different background, culture, race. We were inexplicably bound by a common intention. He took my hand and it seemed like a miracle.

A beautiful young woman, Beth Robinson, who had come to the Washington SYNCON, was also in Jamaica at the invitation of Peter Bentley. She had her masters degree in international communication from American University and found in the SYNCON process a demonstration of an international communication system. We met her with Peter and suggested she stay on in Jamaica as the field representative for TCFF, helping to organize the Jamaican SYNCON. Beth Robinson accepted this offer, and became the first young person to organize a SYNCON on her own.

We were trying to raise funds. One day John, Beth, and I were picked up by an Alcan plane and flown to Mandeville to meet with Mr. Gagnon, vice-president of Alcan and the Jamaican manager, and Keith Sweeby, public relations chief. Gagnon, about sixty-five, was intelligent and calculating. We explained the concept of SYNCON and what we were trying to do. He stared at me with cold eyes. "Isn't this a bit idealistic? Haven't people tried this before —the Christians, the Communists? Why should this succeed?"

"Because a new history is being born. We now have the science and technology and systems to provide for our basic needs without sacrifice or revolution. We're at a stage of growth where interdependence is a pragmatic reality of survival."

My words didn't touch his spirit, although Keith Sweeby was deeply empathetic. As I looked into Gagnon's eyes, I felt I was looking at a dinosaur. I just hoped he was a dinosaur who would give us money. But he didn't.

The Jamaican SYNCON was held anyway in November 1973. Later I wrote in my journal:

> *The SYNCON worked, that is, it survived its birth, will live, and grow. The participation was small, the organization poor, but the process proved itself viable to the participants.*

Cedric McCulloch, director of the Bureau of Regional Affairs, will coordinate the rural SYNCONs, report to the prime minister, and try to organize a post-SYNCON team to ensure the normalization of the process throughout the country.

The real opportunity for Jamaica and other developing countries, whose political infrastructure isn't fixed, is to invent a synthesis—a system beyond socialism and capitalism that involves the unique potential of the individual in the development of the whole community—what they call "the full-involvement society."

What freedom was to the eighteenth century, wholism will be to the twentieth.

6

Greystone! One of the great mansions of Washington. (The Chinese Communists and the East Germans offered fortunes for it as their embassy, but my sister Jacqueline nobly clung on— someone in the family might want it.)

John and I had decided we needed a "center," and in one of his altered states of action he suggested I ask Jacqueline about Greystone. It was just being used by various friends since she, her husband, and five children were in Stanford, California. John said we should open our new center by September 15, 1973. This seemed utterly impossible in May. We were overburdened; we were doing the work of ten; we didn't have enough money; our organizational problems were pressing—the evolutionary mode of organization hadn't yet emerged.

The Evolutionary Way

---
*We can't just sit here
waiting for Armageddon.*

I called Jacqueline and asked whether she would lend us Grey-stone. She had kept the house for several reasons: one, she and her family might move back, and two, she had always had the feeling I might one day want to live in Washington and enter politics.

My brother and sisters—and, of course, my father—have been the most tremendous support to me, even when they didn't fully understand or sympathize with what I was doing. Their willingness to help, their unqualified love, regardless of specifics, has been one

of the great strengths of my life. Jacqueline leads an entirely different life than I. Her husband is a brilliant lawyer; he clerked for
Supreme Court Justice Harlan; he worked for Archibald Cox in
the solicitor-general's office, and argued government cases before
the Supreme Court. Now he's·teaching law at Stanford. Jacqueline
has dedicated herself totally to the development of her children and
husband. Her growth potential has fulfilled itself in the creation of
her family, but as the children grow up, she's gradually increasing
outside activities. She didn't have to go through the traumatic
break, rebirth, and new life that my hunger drove me to.

Jacqueline asked how I was going to manage, what I was planning to do. She said I sounded very tired—was I really able to
undertake a venture to develop an educational center? Did I have
the resources? My family had obviously grown concerned about
me—with my television purchase, the SYNCONs, and the financial
and emotional burden involved. They started to question my sense
of reality. It's true I was driven to experiment with the process and
the media in a way that was causing me to sacrifice my own sub-
stance; there was no question about it. But I really didn't look on it
as sacrifice. I saw it as a necessary expenditure, even though I knew
at some point this mode of operation would have to change. I
operated on faith that the goodness of this effort would eventually
manifest itself in new forms that would be viable in society and
become self-supporting.

I persuaded Jacqueline I was completely rational, and she
agreed to lend us the house. September 15 was set as the date for
opening the center. John chose the date, as he usually does, apparently arbitrarily, far more quickly than any normal human being
could expect anything like that to be achieved. However, we announced to our friends in our newsletter that we were opening the
center in September 1973—and we did.

Hidden in Rock Creek Park off Connecticut Avenue, Greystone is truly Shangri-la. As you drive up the bumpy driveway (the
gravel has long since washed away) you see on your left an old
carriage house of stone, now being renovated by Bill Adler, a
resident, with Buckminster Fuller-inspired hexagonal structures

nestled in the high grass. On your right is a tennis court. Farther on
is a grape arbor, thick with untended vines, lined with years of old
daffodil greens, and the outlines of a stately walk. Then at the top
of the hill you see the house—a bosomy, loving, Georgian,
"mother-type" house with white pillars, peeling paint, four stories:
cozy, yet grand.

Inside is a lovely stairway, very few chairs, but a fantasy of TV
equipment and exquisite antique tables from my past life. It's a
decorator's disaster area—we didn't have the time! The SYNCON-
sole, our social mission control, is in the foyer. TV cameras, hulk-
ing dinosaurs that lurk in corners, stare at startled visitors with
ugly lens eyes. Rows of kleig lights line the living room ceiling for
video-taping "seminars" with "active colleague" friends from all
over the world who stop in for dinner and talk.

We're a pioneering outpost on new territory. We build our
evening fire to keep warm and hail every pioneering stranger:
Come! Tell us what you've found! What's it like out there? What
have you seen? What do you know? We absorb information like all
pioneers—for life's sake.

Then there are the "residents." *Who in God's name are they?
What are they doing?* visitors wonder, being led through the house
by me—still looking like a Lakeville matron who smiles a lot.

Mike Coffey, the towering, former Black Panther leader from
Los Angeles, is eating in the kitchen; Jerry Glenn, a doctoral candidate in futurism from the University of Massachusetts, in pin-
striped grey, is sitting behind his desk on the phone to Herman
Kahn; Marilyn Joy from SIU, four-foot-ten inches, with long hair
and a tiny face, whom John chose as our "Walter Cronkite," is
rereading script for the "TV Evening News"; Phil Kryst, a twenty-
one-year-old "Polish genius" to whom John taught TV direction, is
under the SYNCONsole—fixing the maze of wires; Susan Bell, a
warm-hearted, organic-food enthusiast, is watering the plants; the
"colonel"—John—is in conference with Dr. Don Tartar, chairman
of the Department of Sociology, University of Alabama, about an
upcoming Huntsville SYNCON; Bill Adler, the SYNCON wheel
builder, is off to refurbish the wheel for the next SYNCON, his long

hair tied back, his handsome, sensitive face looking to me like that of a young Abe Lincoln.

Each resident is "self-selected." We'd met most of them doing SYNCONs. I encountered Mike Coffey while building participation in the Inner-City SYNCON in Los Angeles. We met in a small room with a Mexican-American gang leader and an American Indian who had been in prison for outbreaks of violence.

"What's the difference between you and the rest of the do-gooders?" Mike asked me.

I looked at their intense faces. I was frightened, yet deeply drawn by the combined power of so much suppressed anger. Something gave me the courage to tell the truth—straight, because they were so tough and straight in their language (every now and then a stream of four-letter words comes out of me, just to let them know how it sounds when a lady talks that way; they don't like it). "The difference," I said, "is they're working for better living conditions, but we're working for humanity to become one and to move forward toward universal life—which includes food, shelter, and education, but goes beyond."

The American Indian smiled. "That's what my people think. We're a cosmic people." The Mexican-American tried to remember his people's visions—he'd heard something like this before.

Mike decided to join the committee. Later I told him he looked like an African prince; his bearing, his dignity, his sheer physical beauty, were splendid to behold.

One night Carl Madden, chief economist of the U.S. Chamber of Commerce, came to dinner and spent most of the night talking to Mike. They're in essence both cosmic poets—the Black Panther and the chief economist. But only at a place like Greystone would they be likely to let each other know who they are.

Carl told me the house had a "magic." I believe it's the sense of expectation that something extraordinary is about to happen because of *you!* It really has an influence on people. Attraction to the future pervades the atmosphere. No one came in order to create a more comfortable way of life. Each came because he or she wants to build something new. We felt it our first dinner together at

Greystone. Everyone had been dressing very casually—to put it mildly. Suddenly, without saying anything, Jerry Glenn went home and put on his tuxedo. We unearthed our best clothes from the bottoms of drawers and trunks. They were wrinkled, but the militant garb of protest had disappeared; the style of the sixties was symbolically transformed. We ate together and toasted this effort to start a new community for the future.

A friend from SIU, Wayne Woodman, who had written a poem for the first SYNCON, appeared at the center wanting to represent The Committee for the Future and start SYNCONs throughout the country. He came dressed in the style of the sixties: long hair uncombed, dirty jeans, exotic jewelry. "Wayne," I said, "you can't represent the committee looking that way. You're not wholistic; I identify you with only one part of the SYNCON wheel. You'd frighten people by the way you dress. Inside your head you have the whole picture, so why not *look* wholistic? Then you can go everywhere and attract all elements of society to come together." But he wouldn't do it. He had gone too far; he had become an extreme mutation. Gradually I learned to be authoritative based on evolutionary rather than bureaucratic principles.

There were about fifteen people in residence at Greystone. We didn't have enough money to pay anyone, and no one had enough money to pay us, so everyone moved in—until all the rooms in the house were filled with volunteers. The only ones on salary were Jerry Glenn and a secretary. I hadn't given much thought to the living arrangements. But that evening echoed in my mind, satisfying the old hunger of my past life for an intimate community gathered together by a common purpose. Everyone there shared the vision of the importance of synergy on earth and the desire to develop both mind potential and extraterrestrial capabilities. There was quite a difference of opinion on the spiritual aspects of the movement, however. For example, Jerry Glenn had a revulsion against religion and the word "God"—to him it symbolized passivity and irresponsibility. To others, the spiritual aspects were primary; the process of evolution appeared to be representative of God's will. The beauty of the effort was that it didn't matter whether a person had a secular or a religious orientation. The activity was the same, and the feeling became the same.

We soon developed some course material. Jerry Glenn gave a couple of talks on epistemology, asking people's concept of the nature of reality, how they knew what they knew, bringing out a philosophical perception to most of the residents who hadn't thought in those terms. I gave a course on the evolutionary perspective, on the birth image, on the evolutionary spiral, on the shift papers, and on the meaning of synergistic processes. We invited friends to these lectures, and televised some of them.

To study the "new options," we invited key people at the "growing edge" to spend a Saturday with us, describing their activities: Robert Hieronymous, who founded the first accredited school for occult sciences—AUM in Baltimore; Christopher Byrd, who published *The Secret Life of Plants*; F.M. Esfandiary, author of *Up-Wingers* and *Optimism One*; Eliot Bernstein of ABC News; and several others. Each, except for Eliot, who's in a current profession, was pioneering in a new field. Winifred Babcock gave an all-day seminar on *The Shining Stranger* and the thoughts of Preston Harold. When Beth Robinson returned from Jamaica, she did a video documentary called *The Voice of Harold*, based on the seminar that Winifred had given; this was one of the first television products, other than our live broadcasts, that TCFF produced.

The monasteries at the time of the fall of Rome offered oases of learning, to preserve the knowledge of the past; future communities such as ours are now the new places of communal effort, to learn how to share resources and build new worlds together.

One day, shortly after the center opened, Jonas called. "I'll be in town next Wednesday for a dinner. Maybe I could see you somewhere afterwards," he said.

"Fine," I said. "Why don't you come here as soon as you're finished?"

He sounded doubtful. "It'll be after eleven."

"That's all right; we'll be up." I grinned to myself.

I assigned his book *Survival of the Wisest* to the residents, and each reported on a section during dinner. Marilyn Joy summarized the essence:

Human society is undergoing a shift from "Epoch A" to "Epoch B," implying not only the limitations of population growth but a profound shift in values from competition to coalescence, requiring a "double win" rather than "win-lose" or, at least, "nontotal loss" by either element. "Something must be gained by *both* elements of the complementarity even if it is only continued existence, or continued survival in the evolutionary scheme of things."

I pointed out that this "coalescence" and all-win approach is the essence of the SYNCON process. We were primed for his visit!

I put on a long dress and a little mascara. As I went to answer the door, the scene ten years before in Lakeville flashed through my mind. What years! I'd come through alive and was at the be ginning of a new life. The bright light of joy was turned up all the way as I opened the door. "Jonas, how nice to see you!" He kissed me on the cheek and looked around; I waited in silence while it sank in.

"Barbara! What have you here?"

"A launching pad, Jonas! We're educating ourselves. Let's talk a few minutes before you meet everyone." ("Everyone" was waiting for him in the living room, the cameras ready.) I took him into the small, intimate library. "You see, Jonas, a new thing has to begin a new way. People can't coalesce attached to hierarchical, dying institutions—too much negative energy. We're groping toward a new form of organization and education for this age. It's not clear yet, but it's based on attraction to the future and sapiential authority. When you *know* you lead, and when you don't know you follow. There's no 'boss,' no employer. The evolutionary process is in charge; it's up to us to try to understand it and also understand how the forces of change really work—and then work with them."

He nodded, saying, "That's right, that's right," and gave me a biological analogy.

"We'd better join the others," I said, and led him into the living room, introducing him to the residents. "Jonas, would you mind if we televised your talk?" He was surprised, but agreed. However, when they turned on the terribly bright lights I couldn't stand it. I was afraid it would distract him too much, so I made them turn the whole TV system off. John was furious with me, but I told him we had to learn not to let the media destroy spontaneity.

Jonas explained his theory and very kindly offered to spend more time with the residents, to teach them in depth so they could have a deeper intellectual base for their work with the committee. But, much as we appreciated his wisdom, we sensed he didn't share our attraction for the next step. We parted somewhat awkwardly— everything in the air, no commitments made. The impasse had occurred once again, with the vision of the future. He thought I was advocating a break with the past, while in fact I was hungering for the continuity of life.

That very evening, during cocktails and dinner, another of the country's leading thinkers dropped in—Willis "Bill" Harmon of the Stanford Research Institute in Palo Alto, California. We crowded into the study during cocktails, probing him for his vision of the future.

"Catastrophe!" was the word. Bill said he had come to feel the needed changes wouldn't occur until there had been a major breakdown in our economic-social system. Society would probably have to feel deep pain before the shift of behavior from competitive to cooperative could occur. We questioned him sharply about the inevitability of breakdown.

"Bill," I said, "there must be *some* way to avoid this. We can't just sit here waiting for Armageddon."

He agreed. "It's true, Barbara, we have to do everything we can to avoid it, but I really don't think we can. The bureaucracies, the inertia, the patterns of selfish behavior, are so ingrained."

"How do *you* feel about this, Bill?"

He looked very composed. "Well," he said, "the success of humanity isn't inevitable—maybe a better species will come along. We're not indispensable to the universe, you know."

The residents protested. They kept asking again and again: What are our best chances of going into the next phase without disaster? But he seemed to have accepted a Buddhist-like approach —somewhat detached.

I said, "Bill, you may be right, who knows, but we can't operate as though breakdown is inevitable. Our thinking will make it so. Our effort may be decisive." He didn't disagree, but he didn't seem emotionally involved either. Maybe he's worried so much he simply refuses to be upset again.

---

*I hover on the brink
of deeper contact with
universal consciousness.*

It was the Christmas season 1973, as usual a time of agonizing reappraisal for me. It was to be my last Christmas in Lakeville.

> *We've sold the big house in Lakeville and must be out by March. Earl is moving his studio to the hill beside the apple orchard, where my beloved "thinking chair" and apple tree still stand, a memorial to the decade of my silent, total search for purpose, while living amidst the sublime beauty of the Berkshire Hills.*

Lloyd was going to live with us full time at Greystone. Wade was to go to Taft—a boys' preparatory school in Connecticut. Stephanie and Suzanne would use Greystone as a home base during holidays. Alexandra had just called me from Milton, where she was a junior. She was a very independent, strong-willed girl and had been thinking of running away, she later confided. Her best friend had said, "Call your mother; she'll understand." Thank God, she did call. Alex said she was "dying at Milton," unable to do the work that interested her. She wanted to perform certain experiments with animals and wasn't permitted to; her independent work simply wasn't of interest to the faculty. She found no kindred spirit, and didn't like the attitudes of the teachers or students; most of the girls and boys spent their time trying to *break* the rules in petty ways and most of the teachers had to spend their time reacting, trying to *enforce* the rules in petty ways. She asked if she could come to Washington and "study at the Smithsonian."

I immediately sympathized with her, remembering my whole experience at Rye Country Day School and Bryn Mawr. School may be one of the most difficult places in the world to learn anything in this age. "You come to Washington," I said, "and we'll work it out. I'll explain it to Miss Johnson (the headmistress). You're only a junior in high school, though, and you should have some kind of academic connection, so you should leave Milton with a good relationship. But I understand—let's find out what to do."

We all gathered after that—Alex, Suzanne, Stephanie, Wade, and Lloyd, with Earl and me—for the last time in Lakeville, Connecticut. My life had already transformed totally; I had disconnected from my past. It was a strange feeling to walk through the house, the apple orchard, the garden, looking at those sites and symbols of the past, where I had sat for hours searching for meaning, praying for guidance, hoping for a new life. Now that the new life had come, it had swept me along with it. I felt deep compassion for Earl, but no attachment to that past. I felt as if the house had never been mine. In a curious way, I've always experienced the sense of not belonging permanently anywhere. I didn't belong in Scarsdale; I didn't belong in Lime Rock; I didn't belong in Lakeville. I simply didn't and still don't relate to any geographical site on this planet.

I wasn't nostalgic, sentimental, or unhappy. Actually, I felt relief that I no longer possessed the mansion, for it had really possessed me. I was beginning to throw off desire for material possessions. They had burdened me all those years of taking care of them, but they had never once given me joy. The joy of my life has been in sluffing them off and using them as fuel to fire the evolutionary furnace. In fact, I planned to use part of the money from my house to pay for our preparations for SYNCON '76—our proposed Bicentennial project—just as I had used part of my own fortune to buy the television equipment to advance the cause of the

new media. I was ephemeralizing my security. It has never been a
material thing, but I really learned I was secure through dynamic
action, rather than possession, whether of a house or a husband or
even children. (Although my brother and father protected me from
my own evolutionary hunger, and refused to let me have further
access to my heritage, I'm curiously grateful to them for their action. They saved my life both by contributing to my work when I
was desperate and by refusing to let me commit financial suicide.)

At this time I was in deep financial need, and I went to visit
Henry Hendler—I'd been told he might help. His small, plush
office was in Hollywood, and I sat in front of his desk one morning.
He's in his early fifties, has dark hair, dark eyes, and is suave,
touchy—bright-looking. He had a phone by each ear, and was very
tense, very busy. He kept me waiting about ten minutes, and then
said, "All right, what can I do for you?" That always makes my
heart sink. I didn't want him to do anything for *me*. I plunged into
the subject about the potential of humankind and brought out the
SYNCON wheel. After I talked a few moments, he said, "I didn't
understand a word you said. Speak more slowly." I started again,
and then he broke in. "I don't think any of that's possible."

I got up with a sigh. "I don't think you want to understand
anything about the future, so I won't bother you any more."

"Who are you?" he asked suddenly. I told him about my father
and about my brother who by this time had become a very successful businessman; he knew both by reputation. "Come into the other
room," he said, and began to tell me that there was no hope for
man—that there would be a third world war—that people like
myself were idealistic.

I turned the conversation around, and said, "Mr. Hendler, are
you a success?"

"Yes," he said.

"Are you satisfied?" I asked.

He shook his head. "No." Then he started to talk about himself, his family, his children's search for meaning—which is similar
to all children's search, except they were very wealthy and, I later
learned, extremely beautiful girls. He told me there was no chance

for success of the movement I was in because man is irremediably selfish. But he added, "What you're doing is very beautiful, and I'd like to call my daughter in Geneva and ask her to work with you. Even if it can't succeed, it's still right." (As it turned out, Victoria Hendler did come to work with us for a while, but her father never gave a penny.)

As always in times of desperate need I've been able to turn to my family. I took Stephanie to lunch with my father one day at the Twenty One Club, one of New York's most famous restaurants. Almost everyone you see there has accomplished something, is beautiful, or famous. Stephanie is a very pretty girl. Her grandfather is proud of her and loves to call over his old friends and introduce me as his crazy daughter who wants to go to the moon and Stephanie as the smartest girl in the family. My father was giving Stephanie lectures on his favorite theme—the most important things in life are health and money, and women should behave like "puppy dogs." Stephanie was telling him she thought Americans were obnoxious, greedy, and materialistic, but she practically swooned when Aristotle Onassis arrived at the table next to ours. My mind was elsewhere. I was in a state of panic because we were in debt—I'd been spending my own money to finance the SYNCONs since we couldn't raise enough to cover costs.

I hurried to Louis' office after lunch. He's the most remarkable person. He calmly asked me what I needed, what the problem was. When I said I needed a $100,000 loan, he nodded. "I can help you on that," he said, and called in his secretary. "Make out a check for $100,000," he told her, and shortly handed it to me. I practically fainted. He told me he had no way of evaluating what I was doing, that it looked good, and, in any case, I had had a normal life, had raised five good children, had coped with reality, and now I was developing this idea and he'd like to help me. I was flooded with happiness. There was hope!

Earl had been invited to speak somewhere after Christmas, so I took the children, at Stephanie's suggestion, for a week's vacation in Jamaica. Stephanie had a deep need for security and for the family as a secure entity. It was difficult for her, this separation. So

I took them all to Jamaica, and we rented a little cottage by the sea where the children could enjoy themselves. But I suffered as usual; I've never liked vacations. They're a state of emptiness. All the old anxieties come flooding in. I don't feel that way with John, though, even when we're not working. Every now and then he *forces* me to stop working and fretting, teasing me about my P.W.E. (Protestant work ethic), and *makes* me stay out until two in the morning, listening to music, dancing, talking. I love that because with him the evolutionary reality never stops. To remain stable it seems necessary to be acting together with at least one person you love totally who's committed totally to the same goal. This is probably temporary; there's nothing in our culture to affirm evolutionary consciousness now—no churches, no films, no schools—just a few hidden clusters of activity, and, I believe, a growing hunger rising to the surface in millions of people who as yet are uninvolved consciously in change.

> *I'm literally dying to get back into action. I struggle to maintain a sense of evolutionary reality in an environment that in no way acknowledges it. It must have been a comparable experience to be an early scientific observer in a monastery where all action was thought to spring from the unknowable mind of God through laws unreachable by the human mind.*
>
> *Neither mystical nor secular forms of consciousness, which preceded evolutionary consciousness, expect to transcend the human condition through real-time conscious action commensurate with the evolving processes of the universe.*
>
> *I personally hover on the brink of deeper contact with universal consciousness. I suppose it will come forth through the dream realized—through the synergizing earth.*
>
> *Our plan, now called SYNCON '76, is to try to generate a SYNCON in every state from 1974 to 1975, then to encourage their replication through 1975–76 in as many congressional districts as possible, aiming at a national-global*

bicentennial SYNCON from June through August 1976 via communication satellite, to be held at Kennedy Space Center. Shirley Patterson, head of the Horizon's section of the American Revolution Bicentennial Commission, has said she'll staff and present our SYNCON proposal as one of the nationally approved bicentennial programs. She described her meeting with John and Warren Avis and me as a "religious experience." Dad has said he'll sponsor a dinner in New York to initiate the national program. I see the dinner as a celebration of genuine hope in every field of the SYNCON wheel and a kick-off for the "politics of transcendence," the actions necessary to obtain the new options for humanity now.

After our holiday together, the two girls stayed on for a few more days, and I took the boys to Washington with me for a New Year's Eve party. With the coming of 1974, the action we'd initiated was underway. It was halting, a little uncertain in its form, but the SYNCON process, the new media, the center, the active colleagues, the outreaches of various kinds, began to have a dynamism of their own.

With a new year upon us, I renewed my desire to bring together the pieces of experience in an intellectual context. Ideas began to coalesce in my head very rapidly. In Jamaica, I had sketched a book, *The Politics of Transcendence: A Platform for the Future.* I began to have synthesizing thoughts, and I was longing to write a book. But John kept saying it wasn't time, because when I write I become abstract. It's true. In attempting to define ideas, I become academic and lose the joy and reality of the evolutionary purpose. I forget "the story."

Along with the need to provide the conceptual whole in a communicable form, my motivation for empathy and contact with the force that was motivating me grew. I began to sense myself increasingly as a vehicle that had no personal desire for anything other than the fulfillment of this larger effort. I had become so totally identified with the process that I had lost the need for identification with anything personal. You might say I had no personal life—only evolutionary life. To me this state was exciting, natural. I was maturing to a level, however, where I wanted to be free from some of the organizational burdens of how to organize SYNCONs, how to handle the various residents, what to have for dinner, who would clean floors; yet I couldn't escape those requirements. We'd been developing an evolutionary life-style at the center, and even though I was ready to move to a conceptual, evolutionary state of consciousness, I was still confronted with the day-in, day-out maintenance of human life.

We've developed a system for running our operation that borders on an evolutionary organization. Menial tasks are shared. Authority emerges through knowledge in specific fields. I felt strongly that we shouldn't develop a mandarin class. I began to think about Mao Tse-tung's revolution and the natural tendency of certain people to think they're superior to others in all ways and to want others to serve them. So we developed a rather inefficient system—each week one person, by alphabet, is kitchen manager; everyone takes turns cooking by alphabet; we try to share the shopping; and we're supposed to share the cleaning. The result is a messy house and an occasional slip-up at dinner! But the deeper reward is that people are learning to trust one another in a new way. The sign of leadership is a willingness to accept responsibility to act responsively. It's not high intellect or brilliance or charm, although all such virtues help. The group is taking shape on the basis of a person's willingness to accept responsibility for the *whole* action, not just for his or her specific part in it.

The horrible anxiety of debt and financial crisis was gradually being overcome by the work of this evolutionary team. We were generating a "positive cash trickle," as John called it. People were asking *us* to do SYNCONs—from the Federal Energy Administration, to the General Federation of Women's Clubs, to the American Society of Information Sciences; even the White House wanted to engage us to consult on a national youth conference. The young people became expert video camera people. We paid our monthly mortgage on the cameras and televised the president, football games, anything and everything, to earn our living—in order to be free to initiate our own projects. All that I had accepted as a child—affluence earned by others—I was now forced to learn to do myself. And what a joy! It's as though nothing can really be left out of the learning process if we're really to grow. I began to honor money as energy to work for humankind.

We often question ourselves about the rewards: why are we here? The answer isn't always clear. One evening we asked each other: What would we do *personally* if The Committee for the Future should earn a lot of money, either through an enormous grant or through contracts. How would each person spend a personal income over and above committee work? There was silence until one young man, Jack Frost, said he'd like to fly an airplane more often. Beth Robinson wanted to travel more frequently. Bill Adler wanted more equipment for building. Alexandra wanted more material for her art. Many couldn't think of anything except more opportunity to develop themselves through the work. They wanted better television equipment, more access to the media, a chance to do TV productions we couldn't do because we didn't have the money. Those things we wanted to spend our personal money on were minimal in importance compared to the greater desire for self-development through action. A new reward system was clearly emerging, or people wouldn't feel that way. They wouldn't be there, because every one could get a job; some might be able to earn a good deal, in fact. Of course, they were learning skills with us in media, process, futures, that would suit them for many jobs, but they were building no security, career, position, required for survival in the current world.

Even though we were learning to cooperate, I continued to have difficulty bringing evolutionary leaders together for cooperative action. Early in my life, when I met Jonas, he spoke of the mutants and the "invisible college" forming around the world. We met at that time as *individuals*. There was excitement, empathy, joy, but when each of us set out to build new institutions and actions in society, we went through a phase of differentiation and difficulty in cooperating. Maybe it's because each of us is so totally burdened with the effort to establish a foothold, that no one has the excess energy to share it with anyone else. The funding sources are limited, too, and the bureaucratic structure doesn't respond. The number of human beings willing to dedicate their lives to evolutionary action as opposed to revolutionary action is a tiny minority. It's one thing to empathize personally; it's another to develop organizational activities that can synergize. Almost every one of us—Jonas Salk, Julius Stulman, George Land, Jean Houston, Winifred Babcock, Bucky Fuller, Warren Avis, ourselves—is using as much energy as possible to establish the new beachhead.

Even though intellectually I understand the difficulty of cooperation at this stage, the hunger for empathy, deep communication, and working together remains. I can't overcome it, so it's real. I've learned *when the hunger is real, it's satisfiable.* The hunger of Eve that drove me from one pattern to another has proved to be right, satisfiable, natural, normal, good, thrilling, at each step. Whether it be for community, for action, for thought, for the way, in a seed-like form at this stage, every aspect of that hunger was realistic. The idea that the desire for deeper meaning was unpragmatic has proved to be incorrect—look at the so-called pragmatists running the institutions, the cities, and the bureaucracy, failing to meet their own needs and those of their fellow humans. The hunger *is* pragmatic; the food *is* real; the nourishment tastes *so* good. A stage is coming wherein the empathy will flower rapidly; I feel it intuitively. If we're going to make it, humanity will have a stage within the next few years in which the capacity for empathetic organization will be manifest. I intend to do whatever I can to help make that happen.

Ever since I wrote, "I'm a magnet feeling the attractive power of another magnet," I've been drawn by a real force toward this new life. From the awakening of the hunger in Scarsdale to the confusion in material life with my husband, children, and home, to the first nourishment of the hunger through contact with evolutionary people, to the epiphany of the oneness of humankind and our birth toward universal life, to the totality of commitment to an evolutionary way of being, I've followed the pull at the core of my solar plexus. Each phase has grown naturally from the next, never denying the past but rather fulfilling it.

My children are imbued with a strong motivation to grow also. The girls are becoming artists. Suzanne is studying the art of weaving in Sweden now. Stephanie is striving to put her loving spirit into images. Alexandra matured at the center, skipping her senior year of high school, passing through her freshman and sophomore years at American University's Learning Center with straight A's, while doing all the graphics for New Worlds Video and getting a job at ABC-TV News in Washington doing graphics for their evening news show. At eighteen she had decided to take a year away from school and had driven across country with a friend in her little Toyota to Los Angeles, to try her abilities in the competitive world of television. She's earning her own living now, working with Dr. John Lilly in his study of communication with dolphins.

It practically broke my heart when she left. I miss her presence deeply. For all my own breaking with the past, I can't stand to be separated from those I love. She just wrote: "I know you're uneasy about my being out here, but please have faith in me and you'll soon know it was an important step in my development. I'm here in answer to inner drives. If I can't trust these drives I'll never be at peace with myself. I don't know why I'm explaining this to you, though—someone who lives it every day." She's trying to synthesize her interest in art and science, and asked for Jonas' number. (He recently married an artist—the former mistress of Picasso.) Alex ended her letter, saying, "I have a great deal more to accomplish out here, but only till I can move into another phase."

Wade left Taft. He and Lloyd are living at the center now, going to Georgetown Day School. At sixteen Wade is a philosophical businessman, earning money painting houses and setting up the New World Sandwich Service at G.D.S. He was accused of being a capitalist the first day of business and is now figuring out the morality of capitalism versus socialism. Last night he talked for hours with me about the evolutionary entrepreneurship we're developing at the center based on motivation to facilitate the next phase of evolution—our own and humankind's. Lloyd, who's thirteen, has decided on something quite different. He wants to be a pro-football player and go to U.C.L.A. He saved his allowance to buy weights and every afternoon we jog together, I in a half-hearted attempt to "stay in shape," he with visions of glory dancing in his head; he runs ahead, jogging in place, waiting for me.

Earl is living the same life of devotion—painting and writing. The children visit him and say he's radiant, the tensions gone. There's no doubt I was a burden on his soul. He wanted to "make me happy" while I yearned for total involvement in life—and found it. John and I are evolutionary partners now in a new relationship of transcendence. Instead of vowing to remain faithful till death do us part, we've pledged ourselves to give all we have to help humankind toward universal life.

My father, Louis, Jacqueline, and Patricia are all flourishing. Dad sold Louis Marx and Company to Quaker Oats and at eighty presides over his children and grandchildren like a patriarch, judging everyone, loving us. He wishes I had more "status," a job, some recognizable position. "My God, Barbara, you've been at this for years—you ought to have *something* to show for it!" When he takes me to lunch at the Twenty One Club, there's no snappy way to introduce me to those aging friends of his who wave and blow kisses as he comes in. It used to be, "This is the daughter who speaks French." Then, "She's the one who wants to go to the moon." But now—? I think he knows my hunger is related to the drive that brought his own mother across the sea at sixteen, and to the drive he had as a boy in Brooklyn—the aspiration to work toward the highest level of freedom and growth he could imagine. I was just lucky to be born at the time when the energies of past civilizations gathered into a concentrated force to break through the cocoon of earth and lift us toward the new age.

At times of high excitement my thoughts are irresistibly drawn to politics.

We submitted the proposal to the American Revolution Bicentennial Administration (ARBA) for SYNCON '76, but didn't hear from them. They were constantly being reorganized; anyone we made contact with usually retired immediately to some other position. We decided that, with or without the approval of ARBA, we'd organize SYNCON '76, raise the funds, and find a way on our own. (Those who want to do it will do it.) However, late in 1974 we finally received national recognition from them. The vision of the International SYNCON was that people from different cultures and regions and functions of the world would meet at the Kennedy Space Center in light of the growing capacities of humankind as a whole to identify common goals for the future based on the broadest horizon of choices. Television would link people globally for a shared experience of oneness—a step toward the "synergizing earth."

Meanwhile, the theme of "politics of the whole," to bring together the various parts of the body to realize the potential of the whole, had been pounding in my head ever since Jamaica, where the leadership level was eager to experiment with a new process in politics. Then a critical event occurred when I was invited by the Church Women United to their international conference in Memphis, Tennessee, in October 1974. The theme was "The Journey to Wholeness." Margaret Shannon, executive director, had asked me to serve as responder and "synergizer"—to help bring the conclusions of the various task forces into some wholistic perspective.

My turn came at 11:30 P.M. Exhausted myself, and recognizing the exhaustion of everyone else, I raced through my statement to the hundreds of women from all over the world: "The journey to wholeness requires wholistic action. You must go *beyond* adversary politics toward a 'politics of the whole.' The diverse parts of the body must aim at a solution to their own needs that doesn't hurt other sections of the body, that ideally enhances every section's development. A 'Platform of the Whole' should be developed out of the politics of the whole. The Church Women United should take the leadership in both the politics and the platform of the whole. Anyone interested in 'Assemblies of the Whole,' please meet with me directly afterwards."

I don't know exactly how many women congregated, but I

estimate that as many as a hundred wanted to meet, even though it was 11:45 P.M. Our place of meeting wasn't even certain; some waited in the lounge until 2:00 A.M. Their receptivity triggered in me a profound desire for a more overt role of activation. I was charged with excitement. The cells in my body seem to have more electrical energy as I got nearer to the incorporation of action into the whole body.

I left the women in Memphis full of love. Immediately upon landing at National Airport in Washington, I took a taxi to rejoin our New Worlds Video crew who were video-taping a motorcycle race at Rosecroft Racetrack (one of our efforts to earn our daily bread). When I asked the taxi driver to take me there, he looked askance. I didn't strike him as the type who usually attends motorcycle races, and I think I was still wearing my Church Women United badge. When I arrived I plunged into a totally different atmosphere, one of competition, disorder, dust, noise, screeching young people, men hawking flags, popcorn, and other tawdry items. Alexandra was operating a camera on the grandstand. Lloyd was pulling cable in the pit. Everyone was covered with dirt.

I stepped gingerly toward the racetrack, having a horror of the needless risk of life. I don't like horizontal speed; it's dangerous. I forced myself closer to watch the young men going ninety miles an hour, risking their lives at every turn. One pebble could cause death. All at once this willingness to risk life for the sake of breaking a limit, combined with the profound love of wholeness expressed by the Church Women United, caused a chemical reaction in me. Wholeness and risk-taking fused. Suddenly I had a powerful inner commandment: *You must take a risk to create a more wholistic world.* It threw me into a state of great agitation and contemplation, but I couldn't relate to the racetrack and felt disoriented.

I rushed over to John: "I *have* to talk with you," I said. "We *have* to leave—now. Let's go to dinner, alone, so we can talk." My words were sharpened with urgency. We drove directly to a restaurant, leaving the young people to return to the center. "Something's happened to me," I said. "I know I *have* to do something, but I'm not sure what. The fact that the women responded so quickly to the suggestion of Assemblies of the Whole and creating a Platform of the Whole makes me believe the social body is ready. What could I do—what act—to offer the option of wholeness-in-action to the body? The motorcycle races made me realize that risk-taking is part of it. I can't trigger this act—whatever it is—without taking some risk. It's inherent in the body of humankind to take risks; that's as much a part of our nature as love." I kept repeating to John, "I *have* to do something; I feel it's there to be done; I know it can be done; I *have* to do something about it." John said nothing. He just listened in a state of acute receptivity. As always happens to me at these times of high excitement, my thoughts were irresistibly drawn to politics, because politics is the best way to translate ideas into action.

It came over me with a wave of certainty from within that I should run for the presidency of the United States in 1976. This is the first time the idea came from within *me*, although the idea itself had arisen several times in the past: when Tom Turner had mentioned it at Southern Illinois University and, before that, when I was promoting Lincoln Republicanism. Each time it was for the same reason—there's a potential within people that can be called forth to action to build a humane community. Now I'd added the transcendent element that, as we're called forth to build a humane community on earth, we're at the same time opening our future towards universal development. The act of running for president appeared in my mind as a sacred act. It had nothing to do with ordinary power; it had nothing to do with wanting to be president; it had nothing to do with wanting to become a Republican or Democrat. It had to do with wanting to help trigger the action.

In a state of awed contemplation, we returned to the center. The next morning I was too restless to get dressed and was sitting in my robe in the kitchen, before our usual 9:30 meeting of the New Worlds Center in the basement. It was about 9:15 when I said to everyone, "I want to tell you something." I explained what happened in Memphis, and my experience at the racetrack. "I believe we should launch a candidacy for the presidency of the United States." My heart was pounding.

I looked for some reaction in their faces. I think it was Marilyn Joy who first said: "Far out! Great!" One after the other expressed his feelings. Some were instantly positive; some were cautious; Jack Frost was concerned about which party I would run on—how it could be organized; Bernie Kraska was excited; Bill Adler was ready to go; Jerry Glenn was perched on the last shelf in the back, looking upset, saying nothing—I don't know what he thought. Alexandra just looked amazed. So we left the discussion open, and I spent the next few days telephoning other people to see what they thought.

I didn't tell Suzanne and Stephanie or Wade—the idea actually embarrassed me. It was only "real" when I was in an evolutionary state of consciousness, a state I rarely achieved with my own children, even my daughters who encouraged me, and who had caught the flame themselves. I think my closeness to them as a parent rather than as a person made it necessary for them to maintain some psychic distance. My motivation was so overwhelmingly strong that it obliterated their personalities in my presence. But if the campaign had actually begun, I'm sure they would have been part of it in their own way. I didn't tell Earl either. It would only have caused him further pain. In any case, our communication was at a minimum. I wrote to him about the children, and he sent me kind notes on holidays. There could be no real personal exchange at this stage.

Among those I telephoned was Margaret Shannon. "I want to meet with you as soon as possible. I have something very important to discuss." John and I went to see her at Riverside Church Center. She brought Margaret Sonnenday, the next president of the Church Women United. We went at mid-morning to the large, empty cafeteria downstairs, where I had a cup of coffee and an apple. Margaret was probably expecting me to discuss the Assemblies of the Whole. But when I told her, "I've decided to run for the presidency of the United States," she was delighted: "Wonderful! This is what we need. I'm going to retire in March, and this is something I'd be willing to work on. We need a woman who's not just seeking power to speak about a new way of action for the future." Her acceptance was instantaneous.

I called Al Rosenfeld. "I was wondering how long it would take you to decide to do this," he said. But Carl Madden didn't think it was a good idea; neither did Herman Kahn. "You can't change the rules of the game," Herman said. "You'd have to play the old game—you'd have to join one of the parties." He gave me a quick, pragmatic analysis. "You'd have to become a Republican."

"I can't become a Republican," I said. "I can't become a Democrat either, Herman. The point is to create a *new* politics of the whole."

"Barbara," he repeated, "you can't change the rules of the game."

"We *have* to change the rules." But he *was* right in the sense that I didn't know *how* to change them.

I called Norman Cousins and asked if he would have lunch. John and I met him at his usual restaurant, The Barbary Room, next to his offices at *Saturday Review/World*. Once again, I took a deep breath: "Norman, I've decided to run for the presidency of the United States."

He took my hand, smiled, and said, "Barbara, I believe that, of all the candidates, you're the most pragmatic. You understand better than any of them the new age of interdependence and future orientation. But you lack credibility. What's needed is a major announcement over national television, a twelve-minute statement in which you announce your candidacy, state the case, reveal the supporters and backing you have, at least intellectually and socially —that would be the way it would have to be done. But," he added, "you know what you'll be subjected to personally. I hate to see you expose yourself to something so horrendously destructive and difficult. You'd become the target of so many negative forces. Why would you want to expose yourself to such a terrible onslaught of negativity?"

"I'm really not thinking of myself. I'm not even sure I'd be considered seriously for the presidency, much less win it. I don't think I would. But the courage to do it, if the idea is right, would change history. What better thing is there to get destroyed for than that? I could get killed by a car, walking out on the street after lunch. I don't mind if I die. I don't mind if I'm destroyed as long as I feel it does some good. I don't seek death, and I don't seek destruction—I seek life. But that doesn't worry me. The only thing that worries me is that I'd make the act insignificant by my own inadequacies."

As time went on I spoke with about thirty people. Almost everyone thought it was a good idea at first. But as I plotted and strategized with John and others as to the steps required to make it a reality, I became increasingly distressed. I found myself becoming self-promoting. A friend asked, "What about Jimmy Carter? He looks like a good man," and I found myself saying I was better than Jimmy Carter. That was the last thing in the world I wanted to do—to proclaim myself *better* than Jimmy Carter! I was *different* from Jimmy Carter; we weren't in competition. But I saw I'd *have* to be in competition with Jimmy Carter and everyone else in the field. I found myself becoming self-promoting in the adversary mode, concerned about the organizational aspects of the move, the funding, the institutional interface. My energy level started to drain out of me. It was like Samson's hair being cut. My strength was in the motivation to do something new, but the act of doing it was requiring me to do all the old things.

I couldn't figure my way out of that bind. So I postponed it, never quite putting it out of my mind, feeling that the idea had come to me as a signal that there had to be a trigger act, that the act was connected with the presidency in 1976, that I'd play some role in that trigger, but I'd have to wait and see how and where and why. This type of faith is one I'm learning painfully. There's such a desire for immediacy when a powerful commandment comes from within, but that impatience is immature. It was childish to think I could do something of that magnitude so fast.

In that same month, during the misbegotten effort to build participation and to fund the First International SYNCON, we were invited through the good offices of John Yardley, who had

become director of Manned Space Flight for NASA, to testify before the Outlook for Space Committee. NASA had finally decided
to invite citizens and scientists to express their views on long-range
goals for space.

We had planned for some time to form a "Choiceful Future"
research group of active colleagues to develop a "new worlds"
program based on emerging potential in all fields. The NASA invitation was an incentive to develop the Choiceful Future pro-
posals in time to enter the arena of public discussion by 1976.
Instead of running for president, I decided to put together the
elements of a platform that anyone could run on—a platform for
the future. There's a real vacuum of direction here. Traditional
politicians don't articulate new directions, and the futurists who've
gained public attention are limited in number and scope.

There are two major world views contending for support on
the futurist-political scene, both partially true but dangerously insufficient; either could lessen humanity's chances for an open future. One is the Club of Rome's Limits to Growth, which
considers earth a finite system with fixed resources. I had met
Aurelio Peccei, head of the club, in Bucharest in 1972 at a Futurist
World Congress. I asked him if he had examined Krafft Ehricke's
"extraterrestrial imperative." "Dr. Peccei, it seems as though the
future isn't limited if you consider the universe," I said.

"Madam," he replied, "we've looked at the universe and consider it irrelevant."

I was almost speechless. "Dr. Peccei, that's impossible!"

The second world view, Postindustrial Society, is advocated
by Daniel Bell; Herman Kahn, founder of the Hudson Institute;
and others. Herman believes that by developing carefully in science
and technology, taking into account the new needs for conserva-
tion, pollution, and population controls, it'll be possible to provide
more of the same for everyone on earth, aiming toward a wealthy
world somewhat in the mode of the West. He believes in the
"trickle-down" theory and says things are better now than ever
before. He views the future as a somewhat static, humanistic culture, with emphasis on sensual pleasures, cultism, interest in

gourmet food, aesthetics, and such "exotic adventures as space travel."

Herman told me this while we were relaxing together at Michael Michaelis' swimming pool in Washington. He was sitting on the diving board wearing gargantuan bathing trunks that encircled his enormous girth. He always speaks rapidly and mumbles a stream of ideas and facts with extraordinary brilliance.

"Herman," I said, "to me that view is shortsighted, uninteresting, and blind to real changes. You're not taking into account that we're moving forward in the universe, that the potential of the mind is immeasurable. By the middle of the next century this world could be a global society with interconnecting, interfeeling awareness of its members. We could be living and working in outer space and may well have made contact with extraterrestrial life. There'll be new social models from the communities of people living in space."

"Barbara, you're not stating a likely forecast but an intuitive desire" (which is true) "but then I've never been able to have a 'peak experience,'" he said. "What's real for you isn't real for me."

"I understand that, Herman," I said, feeling sympathy for that lack, "but there's nothing I'm saying that's not technologically feasible. We must take into account *motivation* as part of the energy that creates the future. Your view of human nature is basically materialistic—which has been the dominant mode recently. But there's a far longer history of the primary urge to grow beyond material comfort toward greater awareness. Every time a group of people achieved comfort, some became restless and began to break the walls down, moving forward to overcome some new limitation. That's human nature." I came to the same impasse with him as with many others. He doesn't *see* what I see ahead; he hasn't felt the experience or the magnets.

We had a surprising conversation at the Knoxville, Tennessee, SYNCON. He spent two days with us, starring in the "New Worlds Morning News," working the SYNCONsole with John, surrounded constantly by a group of avid listeners—like a wise uncle. He was seated next to me at dinner one night when I received a note that Joanna Leary, wife of the imprisoned Timothy Leary, had telephoned and wanted to come to Knoxville to present their ideas.

I turned to Herman. "How would you like to hear Joanna Leary?"

"What does she think?" he asked, although I'm sure he knew.

"She and Tim believe earth has undergone its larval stage and is now in the process of metamorphosis toward universal life. The religions were intimations in the cocoon of our coming destiny. They were signals from real higher beings. Tim and Joanna are developing a sort of myth about building a starship to begin a galactic voyage with those who're ready." I explained what I understood of their vision.

Herman said, "Well, that's basically what I believe."

"Herman! Is that true? How come you never say it?"

"Barbara, I'm a plumber. My job is to fix things—basic things. You and I are members of the same religion—different church."

An alternative to Herman's Postindustrial Society and to the Club of Rome's Limits to Growth is being developed by The Committee for the Future and others; we call it "Choiceful Future." This view synthesizes elements of the other two and adds a third—the rapid development of inner and outer space. Choiceful Future takes the evolutionary perspective, views the world as undergoing a natural transformation from earth-only to universal. It accepts the Limits to Growth position of the necessity for conversation of nonrenewable resources, for decentralization, diversity, self-sufficiency, use of appropriate technology, and respect for nature and all people as members of our own body; it shares the goal of planetary consciousness and equitable distribution of wealth. It also accepts Herman Kahn's position that where industrialization can be developed with minor or no damage to the environment, it should continue; that through reasonable growth the basic needs of most people on the planet can be met; and it shares his buoyant faith that human intelligence is equal to human problems and that we, as a species, have been steadily improving in our capacity to care for others.

But Choiceful Future transcends the other views by the expectation of new options. It suggests, with Buckminster Fuller, that through the "emphemeralization of technology"—doing more with less—and the "design science revolution," everyone on earth will have enough energy without revolution or pollution and without the spread of nuclear power plants; it accepts Professor Gerard O'Neill's concept that we can build new communities in space, and provide inexpensive solar energy for them and for earth. It also accepts the ideas of Abraham Maslow, Jean Houston, Robert Assogiolo, and countless others that the mind potential has barely been tapped and can be emancipated to reach levels of creativity heretofore considered the prerogative of genius. It views humankind as a transitional species, a link in a vast evolutionary chain, and the essence of human nature as a constant self-transcendence, stimulated to continual growth in a new spirit of wholism.

The Choiceful Future research group met twice, and Professor Gerard O'Neill of Princeton University came to our second session at Greystone. He's a scientist of international reputation, working in the field of high energy physics. I first read about his activities in the *New York Times* and called him immediately. We had a superb talk. (He mentioned the vital need for a $1,000 research grant to a young M.I.T. student, Eric Drexler. I gave it personally —leverage money for the future!) His appearance at Greystone was highly charged with interest. He arrived with his young and attractive wife toward the end of the afternoon. He's a handsome man, with just a hint of the strange perfection of Mr. Spock of "Star Trek." He had wanted to be an astronaut, and has that sense of bearing, precision, and physical discipline.

Gerry gave a slide presentation on the concept of building communities at the L5 Libration point around the moon. The communities would pay for themselves by producing inexpensive solar energy from space. Evidently the "islands in space" could be designed to be aesthetic with varied climates and new architectural forms. The first could be ready in 1990—in our lifetime! He showed artists' renderings of beautiful earth-like cylinders, with trees, animals, clouds. "We *can* colonize space," he said, "and do it without robbing or harming anyone and without polluting anything. If work starts soon, nearly all our industrial activity could be moved away from earth's fragile biosphere within less than a century. The technical imperatives of this kind of migration are likely to encourage self-sufficiency, small-scale governmental units, cultural diversity, and a high degree of independence. The ultimate size limit for the human race on this new frontier is at least 20,000 times its present value."

I was enthralled. The amorphous hunger of Eve found itself in the presence of a scientist providing a way to develop physical universal life that corresponded precisely with my intuitive sense of the future.

I don't yet have a transitional language to make a link between pragmatic men and new action.

In the summer of 1975 Harris Wofford, a refined, sensitive, imposing man, the president of Bryn Mawr, came to the New Worlds Center. Literally, the first words he said were, "Sargent Shriver is going to run for president on *Building the Earth*, by Teilhard de Chardin," and he handed me the book.

It was Shriver's own copy, dog-eared, underlined, starred, obviously a much-loved text. Harris told me he had spent the previous day with Shriver (whom he had worked with when Shriver was director of the Peace Corps). Shriver had told him not to sleep that night until he had read the book.

I was amazed and telephoned Shriver right away to say I knew he was going to run on Teilhard de Chardin and that I thought it was just terrific. "Where are you?" he asked. "Let's meet." I was surprised at such openness from a man getting ready to run for president. "Believe it or not," he said, "I'm at the Watergate, overlooking Kennedy Center. How soon can you come?"

About two hours later John and I went to his large offices on the tenth floor, the law firm of which Shriver is a member. He was being interviewed by the *New York Times*. His son, from Yale, came out and apologized for the delay. He was a tall, ruggedly attractive young man, with the natural charm I associate with all the Kennedys. Finally we were escorted in. The phone rang constantly. In between calls Shriver managed to turn to us.

"I'm amazed at your interest in Teilhard, because we have the same motivation," I said. "I've always felt the presidency should be motivated by these principles."

"I'd like to run a campaign using television-in-the-round," he said, "asking people to participate in building the platform with me. I don't want to stand up at rallies and wave my arms. I'm looking for a way of bringing people forward to build the earth."

I must have been beaming. "This is amazing, because it's exactly what The Committee for the Future is planning to do." I opened my briefcase and got out the plan for developing SYNCONs throughout the United States. I told him we'd be using television-in-the-round, just as we always do, with the SYNCONs, and that we were developing the outline of a Platform for the Future to be built by the people through SYNCON-like meetings.

"This is spooky," he said. He called in one of his intellectual aides, Dave, who didn't seem to have any of the same feelings, certainly not about Teilhard de Chardin, or interactive media.

I laughed. "I can see, Dave, you're a liberal, somewhat skeptical of the evolutionary potential in humanity."

He smiled and said he was hired to be that way; he had to try to "keep our feet on the ground."

Shriver looked at Dave after I'd expounded in the identical words he uses about Teilhard and politics, and said, "I wanted to prove this isn't a 'Papist plot!'"

Eunice Shriver called while we were in the office, and he said, "Barbara Marx Hubbard is here and she loves Teilhard, too. Here, tell her about Teilhard." Eunice has a voice something like Katharine Hepburn's. She quoted Teilhard for five minutes straight.

I shook my head. "I can't believe it. This is great!"

Shriver, John, and I began to talk about his strategy for the presidency. "I once thought of running myself," I said, "to bring the synergistic process and Teilhardian thoughts to political action. I think it's wonderful that you're going to do it." We developed a rapid empathy that had nothing to do with the realities of his position or mine. "I imagine you're going to have a woman for your vice-president," I said, in all seriousness. He looked shocked; apparently it hadn't occurred to him. His aide looked even more shocked. I said, "It's a shame for two men to run. You really have to have a woman for vice-president. How about me?"

I wasn't fooling at that moment, and Shriver was getting worried. On the other hand, he knew in his heart we were on the same wavelength. In fact, he promptly asked me to join his national committee, and we left with good feelings toward each other.

As John and I thought more about it, we became interested and decided to call on him again to see if the meeting had been real and how deeply he felt about the concept of "building the earth." We also wanted to ask him what he thought about space. We'd decided if he *really* intended to do what he said, that we should go all the way with him. We'd put our media, our fortunes, our lives, and our sacred honor at stake for his candidacy.

I called him again. "Sarge, when would you be free to see us?"

"Barbara, I'm at the office every day, all day. You come whenever you want."

That afternoon John and I were at his office again. We waited quite a while as he was making phone calls, trying to get support from various political figures. The man's humility and openness were most impressive. But my heart sank that Teilhard's vision of building the earth seemed impossible to communicate in those telephone calls. He said, "I'm trying to figure out how to translate Teilhard into the rhetoric of politics."

I told him I'd had the same desire and handed him a speech I'd made at the Choiceful Future SYNCON, called "The Politics of the Whole." He read through it and asked who wrote it. I said, "I did."

"This is fantastic!" he said. "These are precisely the ideas that I have!" He expounded on the concept of a new process for the presidency where people would be invited to interact and discuss on television. Then I pulled out a paper in which I'd described that very idea. "I wonder if you'd do something for me," he said. "We're meeting tonight at 7:30 at Timberlawn with some of my closest aides to draft my announcement of candidacy. Could you be there?"

"Of course!" A chill ran down my spine. From the earliest days our goal had been that a presidential candidate would carry the message of new worlds on earth and in space in 1976. Maybe this was it!

Before we left I asked his views on the space program. He said, "I haven't given it much thought—I think it's a good thing, but there's no way in this current political climate that we could overtly promote it. We have to have a low profile on the space program, even though I agree with you that it's important."

I tried to persuade him that, if properly put, it could be shown to be a new hope, a new transcendence, a new start for the world. But he didn't agree.

As we were walking briskly out together, talking about Teilhard's "Omega point," I said, "You know, Sarge, there's something beyond the Omega point—the beginning of our life in the universe." He looked at me with astonishment, and his aides, who already thought Teilhard was far out, looked even more startled.

That night John and I drove to Timberlawn, just north of Washington. It's a Kennedy-like estate. We saw pictures of such settings many times during Jack Kennedy's era—sprawling lawns, big white houses, swimming pools, young men from Yale and Harvard jogging and playing touch football. Eunice and the children were away. People were clustered in different nooks and crannies of the house, working on various projects. No one greeted us, and Shriver hadn't yet arrived. So we wandered through the house and onto the lawn where I saw a table set for dinner with six or seven men sitting at it. I walked over: "Are you people writing the announcement for the candidate?" They nodded, and John and

I sat down. No one paid the slightest attention to us. They were talking low-level politics—what Kissinger had said to someone; who's getting whose hide today. There were two Catholic priests, a man from Brookings Institute, a Harvard lawyer, a press secretary, and other professionals of that kind. Then Shriver arrived around 8:00 P.M. We had a cook-out dinner served by his son from Yale and his friends in an informal atmosphere that reminded me of the center. It was quite charming and wonderful.

Shriver said he'd like to make his announcement in the form of the Declaration of Independence: first the vision, then the grievances, then the statements of action. There was a superficial discussion of possible grievances. People were searching for an issue that could be as specific as the Vietnam issue; they thought it was economics; "break up the oil companies" was the favorite theme. Many suggestions were thrown back and forth and discarded. Finally I broke in as an outsider and the only woman present. "What's the vision of this campaign?" Dead silence.

Shriver looked at me. "You say what you think it is, Barbara."

I restated his own vision. "This is a time when every man, woman, and child is needed to build the earth. This campaign will call on the people to work with the candidate to build a platform of directions for the future. Together the people can build a new world." Dead silence again. No one picked it up. The meeting went on.

Later Shriver asked his press secretary to get in touch with John to help set up the television process for the announcement of the candidacy and the campaign. This seemed to be a specific that we could work on. But the phone call never came. I wrote a letter by hand to him, trying to reinforce his own vision by our affirmation. "If you'll carry out the campaign theme, 'building the earth,' and truly invite the people to build a platform with you, you can do more good than any leader in the world at this time. For such a campaign, John and I would dedicate our entire efforts." We signed it, pledging our lives, our fortunes, everything.

I received a note back sometime later saying, "Thank you for the endorsement." The Sargent Shriver I had met was gone for the moment, lost in the back-breaking effort of his campaign. We did have some sympathetic conversations with his community program developer, Grove Smith, who responded to the idea of using the synergistic process and television. He invited me to "slip into" New Hampshire, without any official authorization from the candidate or the staff or anyone, to try a few SYNCONs with Shriver people and other citizens to see how it would work. We pondered the invitation. I had always longed to try a SYNCON in a political context. But because there wasn't any response from the candidate or his staff, we decided it would be misusing the process, which had a chance of spreading in a transpolitical mode through the country in the Bicentennial year. We might lose our chance of doing it by identifying with one candidate who wasn't standing up for the wholistic vision.

We weren't invited to help him design his television campaign or his process; however, on their own initiative, the young people of the New World Center brought our mobile television van and cameras to televise his announcement at the Mayflower Hotel in Washington. It was done in traditional style. The press corps was sitting in the center of the crowded ballroom. Supporters and friends, numbering at least a thousand, were jammed in the room. Shriver made a traditional opening statement that had no bearing on the Declaration of Independence, building the earth, or tele-vision-in-the-round. His main point was that he represented the Kennedy legacy. It was an old "New Deal" approach.

Then came the questions from the press. When Beth Robinson, who isn't a member of the press, asked, "How are you going to involve the people in your campaign?" Shriver gave an equivocal answer. Beth was criticized by others in the press because she didn't have a press card.

I was deeply disappointed that his opportunity had been lost, but I try to understand everything as an evolutionary signal. I know Sargent Shriver believes in Teilhard de Chardin and building the earth. I also know the old game of politics has forced him to be silent in terms of his vision. He had said to his press secretary, when we were discussing television-in-the-round for his announcement, "I want to get to the people. Maybe John and Barbara can help me." The press secretary had said, "The *New York Times* will have Johnny Apple and Scotty Reston there. They might think it was a gimmick and make fun of it. We'd be ruined at your first statement." Shriver had said, "I don't give a goddamn about Johnny Apple and Scotty Reston; I want to get to the people." But the fact was, he didn't do the new thing.

This experience with Sargent Shriver, along with my own experience in contemplating running for the presidency, has given me a new sense of inner authority. I believe the next step is going to be taken by nonpolitical people who already have a whole picture in their heads. I used to be distressed by the refusal of the men of America to take initiative. But now I feel it's in the interest of humanity that the existing structures don't lead the way. Those who're taking overt initiative in the development of both inner and outer space are usually working not against but outside the current system and large institutions. It appears the initiative *is* coming from and *ought to* come from people who have no vested interest in current growth patterns. Perhaps once again the mammals will eat the dinosaur eggs rather than confront the prevailing giants directly.

An example of this mammalian initiative occurred in Acapulco in January 1975. One of our active colleagues, Orville Freeman, is president of Business International, an organization that serves and informs the largest multinational corporations in the world. Orville is a pragmatic idealist attempting to bring social coherence to this great worldwide force of development. I had asked if I could address his executive conference of eighty-six chief executives: "Doing Business in a Resource-short World." I wanted to present the Choiceful Future scenario.

When I described the potential for manufacturing and building habitats in space, he said, "Barbara, you blow my mind!" We were in his office in New York. Orville was secretary of agriculture under Kennedy. He's a man of great ability and integrity, with a kind, gentle face. But he had never thought about new worlds, just as most persons in positions of high power haven't. "I'd like to try to get you to the conference," he said. "These are the heads of the most important corporations in the world. But what would you say to them?"

"I'd tell them we're entering the universal age, becoming interdependent on earth and opening immeasurable horizons in the universe, that we have new limits on this planet and completely new areas of development in the universe, but that the development must be done in a cooperative, synergistic manner—or it'll fail."

He said if he could "package" me correctly, so I wouldn't look too different from the rest of them, I could speak. My theme was to be "Beyond the Limits to Growth."

Warren Avis picked up John and me at the airport and took us to his beautiful home in Acapulco where we stayed during the conference, which was being held at the Princess Hotel there.

The meeting began at 8:30 A.M. every day. Long tables were lined in an enormous ballroom and at each chair was a plaque with the name of the chief executive of an international corporation: Olivetti, General Foods, TRW, Mercke, Nippon Steel, etc. Also present were some resource people, such as Peter Drucker, Walter Heller, and Fred Bergsten of Brookings Institute. I was the only woman, except for the wives who were seated at the side of the room, several hundred feet from the long table, on chairs in rows. I felt totally out of place. I'd rather have been with a group of flaming radicals, because at least they're *for* social change.

I didn't know what to say to any of them, and they didn't know what to say to me. We went to a few painful cocktail parties, but John and I rushed back to Warren's house when the meetings were over. We swam in the ocean; Warren's cook made tacos for us; and we talked for hours in the starlight about the future. I became convinced of the need for people like us to become financially independent of existing sources of funding to initiate new worlds' projects.

When the time came for my speech, Dr. Knoppers, a member of the Club of Rome, introduced me as a "historical discontinuity who was going to give them a new insight." There was a bit of guffawing (I was a historical discontinuity simply by being a woman).

I said, "Yes, I'm speaking of a historical discontinuity, gentlemen. Our world is going through an evolutionary shift from the earth-only to the global-universal phase. But I'm speaking to you from my experience as a mother." (This wasn't very well received as a background, but I said, "Motherhood is the greatest experience a woman can have to develop concern for the future.")

Then I described the three world views and said that the Choiceful Future offered the best incentive for nonexploitive growth and the most realistic, enduring incentive for their own development, if they would work together to build the next platform for human development. I also said there are processes of citizen involvement that are liberating the greatest potential on earth—human energy. The hierarchical structures within which people are operating in the large corporations and institutions are suppressing potential. I asked for their initiative in opening their structures to more consensual participation in decision making.

I read from Ted Taylor's article (which he had written in the *Saturday Review* about The Committee for the Future)—he listed resources that could be mined on the moon. The chief executive of the Nippon Steel Company, who had given a talk about the limitation of resources, saying the last remaining resources available were in the ocean beds, looked at me with surprise and wrote down verbatim the minerals to be found on the moon. I spoke of the low cost of providing solar energy from space, the feasibility of manufacturing in zero gravity with no fragile biosphere to damage, and I mentioned O'Neill's concept of communities in space. I called for a ten-year decade of "open worlds development," to initiate the benign industrial revolution, and suggested that the multinationals participate in a concerted effort to identify new options, to formulate and assess action, and to outline strategies to pursue lines of development consistent with their business objectives *and* their objectives as members of humankind-in-transition.

After I sat down, Dr. Knoppers asked, "Are there any questions?" There weren't—I think they were stunned. However, later, when Orville Freeman was making his concluding statement, one man stood up: Simon Ramo, chairman of the board of TRW, one of the largest advanced corporations in the world. He said, "Mrs. Hubbard told us something I believe we should listen to. She told us we're not thinking ahead, that we're limited to the present. I want to support her and call upon us to examine these new options for the future."

When it was over I stood there awkwardly, wondering if I had done any good at all, feeling inadequate. Several chief executives came up, somewhat shyly, and said they'd like to hear more. The head of Olivetti, the president of Mercke, the chairman of the board of Foremost-McKesson, Mr. Wearley of Ingersoll-Rand, and others expressed interest. But I lacked the power to make anything happen directly—my "reality factor" was low.

This is one of the agonies of my particular role. I don't yet have a transitional language to make a link between pragmatic men and new action. I spoke with Sy Ramo later at a party, and thanked him for his comments. "Why are so few of those brilliant men thinking about the *obvious* new horizons?" I asked. "There's nothing I said that isn't fully known. It isn't like Einstein explaining $E = MC^2$ for the first time. We've been to the moon; we've examined the resources; we know the earth is finite. These corporation men are more aware of all of that than I."

Ramo agreed, but said, "The pressures of their work, the competition, the enormity of the organizational task, the significance of every little fluctuation of the stock market, the complexities of the Common Market, working in different nations, are all so great they literally can't lift their heads and survive unless they give everything to the present. I'm the same way. I have no time. I can't think."

We're clearly up against an interesting barrier. The best people, in power positions—Thomas Paine, Al Rockwell, Sy Ramo, Sargent Shriver, and all the others—are prevented by the structures they successfully maintain from taking the initiative to do what they believe should be done. Success in the old system is a barrier to enabling the birth of the new. This leaves the field open to those motivated by pain. But there's almost no initiative in this country for positive steps that hold new solutions for the pain problems, that open new possibilities.

*I'm reaching for
the Tree of Life.*

The need for affirmation of the quantum leap was apparent to me at Arcosanti. The United Methodist Global Ministries Research and Development Board had invited me to be a "resource futurist" to meet with their board and others, including the theologian John Cobb, to view the Arcology being built by Paolo Soleri with amateur volunteer help in the desert near Scottsdale, Arizona. A chapel to Teilhard de Chardin was to be its focal point The question we were asked was: What are the future religious implications of the Arcology and how should the United Methodist Church relate to it?

Paolo had told us he looked upon the evolutionary process as the urbanization of matter—from macromolecules to cells to multicells to humans to cities and now to the next phase of synthesis of complexity—the Arcology. It's a prototype for a new, human, architectural ecology, inviting hundreds of thousands of people to live in close communication with each other, eliminating urban degradation and suburban sprawl, waste of energy in transportation, and misuses of land, and creating a pattern wherein individuals can grow more humane.

John Cobb spoke to the ministers the day after we arrived. He told them "Christian realism" had become insufficient, that "Christianity had to become future-oriented again." He was addressing the criticism of ministers working on the front lines of urban suffering, concerned daily for people living in poverty and disease. The ministers shook their heads in disapproval. They didn't want to give up the care of the suffering. It made them angry even to consider the "diversion" of funds to something that might not work.

"But how well is the Church working in Harlem?" John asked. "Is all the charity of the churches of the world and all the charity of the welfare state sufficient to create a better society?"

Paolo, who was sitting quietly at John's side, said, "Charity on this scale has become naive."

"We can't happily choose to let anyone suffer," John said, "but I'm beginning to feel we have to build something new rather than just try to stop the collapse of the old."

Someone asked Paolo if he was sure the Arcology would work. He shook his head. "No. In biology most mutations aren't viable. The same is true of social inventions. The Arcology is a conscious mutation. It may not work. But, nonetheless, we have to do it, and I personally believe it *will* work. How'll we know, though, if we don't try?"

I was hanging onto every word. "You're in the midst of a quantum leap here," I said, glancing at the ministers. "Paolo Soleri is making that leap."

"What's a quantum leap?" someone asked.

"Have you read about how an electron jumps from one orbit to the next around the nucleus of an atom, and never exists in between? That's a quantum leap. So, in evolution, there's a seeming discontinuity from one mutation to another. Something does occur, but usually it's subtle and hidden. You're in on an evolutionary secret here, listening to Paolo. He's showing you a change that's almost imperceptible now, happening in the midst of the desert, with volunteers. He's building the next level of cooperative habitation for the mutualization of humanity. If you miss it, the Church will miss being part of it—but that's all, because it'll happen anyway. We need a theology of the quantum leap—how to get from here to there." Heads began to nod in understanding.

"We can take the quantum leap *and* minister to suffering during the transition," I said. "Society still has enough energy to do both. There *are* people willing to help where help can be given, and there are those eagerly trying to work on the quantum leaps. We musn't divert the geniuses willing to risk the quantum leaps and condemn them as uncharitable just because they aren't working on immediate suffering. We should understand the great morality and compassion of the people building arcologies, people planning space communities, people trying to understand the aging process, people building laser information technologies and educational satellites. They need spiritual blessing as much as someone assuaging the suffering of the dying on the streets of the world. They're not far out—they're far *in!*"

As I was leaving I caught the eye of one of the ministers. I could see he was weighing my remarks skeptically. Something in his face reminded me of the Jamaican industrialist who had asked why people should succeed now, when so many had already failed: Christians, Communists. How could I make them understand that *no one has failed.* Buddha hasn't failed; Mohammed hasn't; no one! It's simply too early to judge. The time of fulfillment may be at hand, however, for in our age we'll evolve either toward the consciousness of oneness and transcendence, or to some form of death—whether by fire or by ice.

We're really confronted with an unprecedented pragmatic situation: the tools for Armageddon or transformation. We have the tools, and we've always known we have a larger purpose than to eat, sleep, reproduce, and die. The fact that our tools are developed through our minds' capacity to understand and work with the laws of the universe means our new powers are natural. It's *natural* to understand the potential of our own minds. It's *natural* that we can build rockets and leave earth alive. It's *natural* to understand our own genetic codes as we approach new environments in space. It's *natural* that we understand nuclear energy, the power at the heart of matter, as we launch toward the thousands of suns of the galaxies. It's *natural* to build the "androsphere," just as it was for the cells to build the biosphere. It's *natural* to be born into universal life.

Eve was right to eat the apple of the Tree of Knowledge of Good and Evil, and she was right to be curious about that second tree in the garden. For forty-six years I carried this hunger of

Eve—a hunger that drove me out of my own Eden of comfort to search for universal action and consciousness. With every step I followed a compass of joy that led me through the labyrinth of a dying age, until now I've become magnetized myself. My life has transformed completely. I'm neither young nor old, but ageless. I'm in a continual flow of growth. I'm reaching for the Tree of Life.

Some Meaningful Books

Aurobindo, Sri. *Sri Aurobindo or The Adventure of Consciousness.* Pondicherry, India: Sri Aurobindo Ashram Press, 1968.

Avis, Warren. *Shared Participation.* Garden City, N.Y.: Doubleday & Co., 1973.

Bird, Christopher, and Tompkins, Peter. *The Secret Life of Plants.* New York: Harper & Row, Publishers, 1973.

Bronowski, J., and Mazlish, Bruce. *The Western Intellectual Tradition.* A Harper Torchbook. New York: Harper & Row, Publishers, The University Library, 1960.

Bucke, Richard M. *Cosmic Consciousness: A Study in the Evolution of the Human Mind.* New York: E. P. Dutton & Co., 1969.

Cox, Harvey. *The Secular City.* New York: Macmillan, 1965.

de Chardin, Teilhard. *The Phenomenon of Man.* New York: Harper & Row, Publishers, 1959.

————. *Building the Earth.* Wilkes-Barre, Pa.: Dimension Books, 1965.

————. *The Future of Man.* New York: Harper & Row, Publishers, 1969.

222

Ehricke, Krafft. "The Extraterrestrial Imperative." *Arise*, 1, 1972. (Available from The Committee for the Future, Inc., 2325 Porter St., N.W., Washington, D.C. 20008.)

Esfandiary, F. M. *Optimism One.* New York: W. W. Norton & Co., 1970.

———. *Up-wingers.* New York: John Day Co., 1973.

Frankl, Victor E. *Man's Search for Meaning: An Introduction to Logotherapy.* Boston: Beacon Press, 1959.

Fuller, R. Buckminster. *Operating Manual for Spaceship Earth.* New York: Pocket Books, 1970.

Futurist, The. Periodical published by World Future Society, 5501 Lincoln St., Washington, D.C. 20008.

Gabel, Medard. *Energy, Earth and Everyone.* San Francisco: Straight Arrow Books, 1975.

Harold, Preston. *The Shining Stranger.* A Harold Institute Book. New York: Dodd, Mead & Co., 1967.

Hubbard, Earl. *The Search Is On.* Los Angeles: Pace Publications, 1969. (Obtainable through *The Futurist*, 5501 Lincoln St., Washington, D.C. 20008.)

———. *The Creative Intention.* New York: Interbook, 1974.

Huxley, Julian. *Evolution in Action.* New York: Mentor Books, 1953.

Jantsch, Erich. *Design for Evolution: Self-Organization and Planning in the Life of Human Systems.* New York: George Braziller, 1975.

Maslow, Abraham H., ed. *Motivation and Personality.* New York: Harper & Row, Publishers. 1970.

Maslow, Abraham H. *Religions, Values and Peak Experiences.* New York: Viking Press, 1970.

———. *The Farther Reaches of Human Nature.* New York: Viking Press, 1971.

———. *Toward a Psychology of Being.* New York: Van Nostrand Reinhold Co., 1971.

Meadows, Dennis. *Limits to Growth.* New York: Universe Books, 1972.

Monod, Jacques. *Chance and Necessity: An Essay on the Natural Philosophy of Modern Biology.* New York: Alfred A. Knopf, 1971.

Plato. *The Republic.* Translated by Benjamin Jowett. A Vintage Paperback. New York: Random House.

Puharich, Andrija. *Uri.* Garden City, N.Y.: Anchor Press, 1974.

Roger, Carl. *On Becoming a Person.* Palo Alto, Calif.: National Press Books, 1974.

Salk, Jonas. *Man Unfolding.* Edited by Ruth Anshen. New York: Harper & Row, Publishers, 1972.

————. *The Survival of the Wisest.* New York: Harper & Row, Publishers, 1973.

Schumacher, E. F. *Small Is Beautiful: A Study of Economics as if People Mattered.* New York: Harper & Row, Publishers, 1974.

Smuts, J. C. *Holism and Evolution.* 1926. Reprint. Westport, Conn.: Greenwood Press, 1973.

Taylor, Theodore B. "Strategies for the Future." *Saturday Review/ World,* December 1974.

Van Der Post, Laurens. *Jung: And the Story of Our Time.* New York: Pantheon, 1975.

Van Gogh, Vincent. *Letters to Theo.* Garden City, N.Y.: Doubleday & Co., 1958.

Whyte, Lancelot Law. *The Next Development in Man.* A Mentor Book. New York: New American Library, 1948.

Barbara Marx Hubbard was born on December 22, 1929 in New York City and attained her early education in private schools in and around the city. In 1951, after spending her junior year at the Sorbonne in Paris, she graduated cum laude from Bryn Mawr.

She founded, with John Whiteside, The Committee for the Future in 1970, a nonprofit organization dedicated to bringing the positive options for the future into the arena of public discussion and action. The Committee has developed a new conference process called "SYNCON" (for synergistic convergence) which invites diverse elements of society to come together to examine their own needs in the context of the growing capacities of society. She also founded The New Worlds Center, a community for the future in Washington, D.C., where she now lives with two of her five children.